GINO

A CHILD OF WAR

GINO
A CHILD OF WAR

DOUBLE‡DAGGER
— www.doubledagger.ca —

WARTIME
W
Friends

Library and Archives Canada Cataloguing in Publication
Wartime Friends, author
Gino: A Child of War / Wartime Friends

Issued in print and electronic formats.

ISBN: 978-1-990644-81-8 (soft cover)
ISBN: 978-1-990644-82-5(e-pub)

Editor: James Leslie
Cover design: Pablo Javier Herrera
Interior design: Winston A. Prescott

Double Dagger Books Ltd
Toronto, Ontario, Canada
www.doubledagger.ca

TABLE OF CONTENTS

Dedicated to all the Canadian soldiers who
fought for the people of Italy
and to all the children who became orphans in the war,
whose memory has been forgotten.

This story wants to be,
ideally, the story of them all.

MYSTERY OF IDENTITY

A whirl of memories and moments
A storm which throws my feelings into confusion.
Like planets colliding
New worlds forming.
This disconsolate soul is suffocated.
Compressed by forces in opposition.
It cries and tosses and turns.
Such great suffering.
Like a leaf floating in the restless air
My soul drifts aimlessly.
Perhaps like this, perhaps because
I do not know what my identity is.

Gino, 1992

FOREWORD

IT WAS MAY 23, 2011, and freelance historian Karen Storwick was in Italy honouring the 67th anniversary of her great uncle's death in the battle of the Hitler Line—as she had been doing for several years. That year, on her annual pilgrimage travelling in the footsteps of Canadians in Italy, her first stop was in the region of Bagnacavallo, near Ravenna. This was where the Canadians fought their last battles in the liberation of Italy. Karen's husband had a great uncle buried at the Ravenna Cemetery, so they visited his grave for the first time. He had been one of the last soldiers to die on Italian soil during the Second World War.

After what was a very emotional day, Karen, and her husband enjoyed a lovely dinner on the patio of Mariangela Rondinelli's home, who had hosted them during their stay. Mariangela is a researcher and an accomplished writer from Bagnacavallo. She helps keep the legacy of Canadian service and sacrifice alive through Wartime Friends; an organization that fosters acts of remembrance rooted in the Second World War.

Once the dishes were cleared, animated conversations filled the air. Mariangela then revealed to Karen that she and her research team were working on a very important project—the story of Gino, a little orphan boy who had been adopted by Canadian soldiers during the war. So far, she said, they had a photograph and just a few details. Understanding he was from the Province of Frosinone, they wanted to find out if he was still alive, in the hope of eventually piecing together what they believed was a remarkable story.

Karen had some friends and colleagues, researchers and historians, working in the Frosinone area, and wondered if they could help Wartime Friends' quest for more information about the boy. On her return to Canada, she informed her contacts in the Frosinone area about Mariangela's research and pursued it no further at the time.

Research projects can take time to complete or end up being abandoned for any number of reasons. Such was not the case for this project. Wartime Friends applied their exceptional investigative skills to the task and diligently pressed on.

Coincidentally, in late 2012, when Karen reached out to two of her research friends from Frosinone, they had a very exciting story to share with her. Incredibly, it was about Gino—the same destitute Italian boy Wartime Friends had been trying to identify. In fact, one of the researchers, Paolo Sbarbada, had located Gino's baptism certificate in the archives of a local church. The research circle was complete, and now Gino, who had lost his identity many years ago during the war, had discovered it again. By now 74 years old, it seemed, he had truly been re-born under a lucky star. Karen became immersed in the story again, helping Wartime Friends edit English transcripts as the story was written.

There is another layer to this story as well. Giovannangelo Battista lived in the small town of Casalciprano, in the Italian Province of Campobasso. Shortly after the Second World War broke out, he was drafted into the Italian military. After Italy surrendered on September 3, 1943, Giovannangelo was among those immediately taken to a German prison camp. When the town was liberated by Canadians the following year, local authorities wanted to show their gratitude for the remarkably friendly care provided to the citizens by the Canadian liberators. Symbolically, they unofficially renamed Campobasso "Canada Town," a name that was preserved for the remainder of the war. After his release, Giovannagelo returned to his hometown, married, and started a family. One of his 5 children was named Tony.

Following the war, when Tony was ten years old, his whole family immigrated to Canada and settled in Montreal. Tony eventually joined the Canadian Armed Forces. Some thirty-eight years later, and after a year in Afghanistan, Tony was posted to Rome as the Canadian Defence Attaché to Italy.

Shortly after his arrival in Rome, in the summer of 2012, Tony was handed an invitation from Gianni Blasi (a teacher, historian, and researcher on the Second World War, living in the province of Frosinone) to an event that would take place on December 16, 2012 in the small town of Torrice, which was Gino's birthplace. The ceremony had been organized with the express purpose of acknowledging Gino's identity and his remarkable wartime story.

Gino did not have a birth certificate or other documents. He went to school but could not be officially enrolled because no one knew his real name, date or place of birth. He was a real person but, in legal terms, he did not exist. In 1954 the local court in Ravenna gave him the name of Gino Farnetti (unfortunately with a double "t," instead of his adoptive family name, Farneti). Ten years after he was rescued, Gino finally did legally exist, albeit with an adopted name!

During the ceremony, Gino was presented with his original baptism certificate – proving his true birth date (26 April 1938). For the first time, he now knew he was 74 years old.

Gianni Blasi, Mariangela Rondinelli, other local researchers – Paolo Sbarbada, Costantino Jadecola, Maurizio Federico and Alessandro Campagna, as well as the mayor of Torrice, Ernesto Raio, the Prefect of Frosinone, , Eugenio Solda, and many others were in attendance. It was here that Tony met Gino and his lovely wife Rita for the very first time. Tony was captivated by Gino's story.

Following the event in Torrice on December 16, 2012, Gino and Tony became best friends and continued to meet many times, both in Italy and in Canada. Seized by this compelling story, Tony suggested they work together to produce a film about Gino's story. Humbled, Gino vowed to support Tony's dream on condition the film honour his Canadian guardian angels by showcasing—to their families, to future generations of Canadians, to Italians and, indeed, to the world—their amazing kindness.

The idea quickly gained momentum and on May 4, 2013, Gino and Tony were again together in Torrice and Frosinone, meeting with a small group from Canada that included Karen Storwick. This was the very first time Karen and Tony met and, fortuitously, it occurred in Gino's presence! It was through her talents as a cinematographer and project manager that Tony's dream to produce a film of Gino's story and his guardian angels would eventually come true.

Fast forward to 2022 when Tony reached out to Karen and her Combined Forces Production team, including talented film director Robert Curtin, about the possibility of documenting Gino's story into film. They accepted and unreservedly rose to the challenge. Tony, whose multi-year efforts to find a film company to collaborate on this project finally succeeded!

Gino's story represents the best of humanity. It demonstrates the incredibly strong will to survive during what was, arguably, the greatest calamity the world has known. As we continue the study of war in search of knowledge and lessons on how to mitigate and hopefully avoid them, we are shocked by the unfathomable devastation, sheer destruction, and brutality that humans can inflict on each other. Those of us who have been impacted by war on a personal level understand the power of emotion triggered by the discovery of even small details that led to piecing together amazing stories from this not-so-distant past.

Gino's story triggers such emotions and serves as a bridge between Italians and Canadians. It points to strong bonds whose roots run deep because of events and actions that occurred during the Second World War. It is a poignant reminder of the human experience, binding us beyond borders.

Many Canadians who have had relatives answer the call to serve in the Second World War, for a cause that was not only just but crucial to the survival of human decency and compassion, feel the need and, yes, the duty to remember them. Sometimes this is by rereading pages in a diary and looking at long forgotten medals. Or it might be by looking through photos of those proud and handsome young soldiers in newly issued battle dress, or by visiting a cenotaph in their honour.

They were called "The Greatest Generation" because of their unfailing demonstration of self-sacrifice for the greater good. Many of them were still in high school or working on a family farm, and would have been excited about the adventure they were embarking on. It is also true that, almost without exception, they willingly walked away from loved ones and the comforts of home to be part of something greater, the preservation of a certain way of life. They witnessed the horrors and scars of war, confirming what they had perhaps heard from their fathers and relatives who had marched off in 1914.

Gino's story touches many Italian and European families. It reminds them of the terrible tragedies their towns and villages were subjected to. It rekindles memories of occupation, fear, and starvation. It also reminds us that these tragedies occurred not so long ago, and that we are in constant danger of forgetting that they really did happen and, sadly, continue to happen!

It is also a tribute to the dedication and perseverance of many quiet researchers, like the Wartime Friends group, who are passionate about not allowing us to forget the sacrifices of so many, and providing Gino, his guardian angels, and their families the gift of healing and closure.

At long last, the book and the companion docu-drama film, chronicling the story of Gino Farnetti Bragaglia and his Canadian guardian angels from the Second World War will be unveiled. Wartime Friends initially chronicled their research in a 2012 book called "Il Bambino in Divisa." Through further research and collaboration, both in Italy and Canada, the English version of this book, and its companion film, entitled "Gino: A Child of War" were born.

Gino is a thankful man; he is at peace; he is grateful. The book and the film are a tribute to him and to his guardian angels. Their incredible journey of survival, courage and hope is one that, in many variations, was forced upon hundreds of thousands of innocent families in the third and fourth decades of the 20th century. This is a story of human dignity, respect, and hope. Born out of the ashes of war, this story has now come to light to be preserved for present and future generations.

As one can imagine, many more people were involved in the telling of this story, captured in research and interviews conducted by Marco Battista over the past several years. Marco added much documentation to the Gino story and his guardian angels, through extensive interviews with Gino, Mariangela, Gianni Blasi, Paolo Sbarbada, the families of the Canadian soldiers who saved and nurtured Gino, and many others. Marco also put together an initial short documentary that eventually became the genesis for the professional film.

Readers will no doubt be fascinated by how the book documents the amazingly diverse series of "fortunate" events that have followed Gino and his Canadian friends, beginning with the days of his rescue and continuing for many years since his true identity was recovered in 2012.

The book and film are also a tribute to the human values of Canadian sailors, soldiers and airmen and women. They crossed the ocean to fight against the terror of an evil regime; they displayed humility, compassion, dignity. They extended care to their fellow human beings. This is still true today, and something for which we can be most proud.

Let us remember to teach these values to future generations.

Karen Storwick and Tony Battista

THE CANADIANS IN ITALY

DURING THE SECOND WORLD WAR, the first contingent of Canadian soldiers landed in Italy on the south coast of Sicily overnight between July 9 and 10, 1943. From the beaches of Pachino to the Strait of Messina, the Canadians advanced up the boot of Italy, fighting and leaving many dead on the ground.

By October they were in Campobasso before their move over to the Adriatic and the long hard fight along the Sangro and Moro Rivers. By the end of December, the Canadians had liberated the town of Ortona.

Between January 20 and March 25, 1944, the Allies repeatedly attacked the German Gustav Line around Montecassino, in southern Lazio. The aim of the offensive was to meet up with the beachhead forces which had been established at Anzio and then to converge on Rome to liberate the capital, which was still occupied by Nazi troops. The Allies' plans were slowed down by strong German resistance around the town of Cassino which, along with the ancient abbey situated at the top of the nearby mountain, was destroyed during heavy bombing and artillery fire on February 16.

The Allied winter offensive finished without having met their objective.

In the spring of 1944, the Germans were still firmly holding the front from Cassino to north of Ortona. In April and May, the British 8th Army, which also included the 1st Canadian Corps, moved in great secrecy to fight alongside the US 5th Army in the battle for the liberation of Rome.

On May 11 the attacks began again, coordinated both by the US 5th Army, which was deployed along the front between the Tyrrhenian coast and the Liri River, and by the British 8th Army, which was responsible for a wider area bordered in the east by the Liri River and the town of Cassino. The 13th Armoured Corps was deployed, consisting of eight divisions and three brigades. Two Canadian divisions (the 1st Infantry

Division and the 5th Armoured Division), and a British armoured brigade (the 25th Tank Brigade) were kept in reserve. However, the 1st Canadian Armoured Brigade, attached to the 8th Indian Division, was instrumental in the assault. Through the ingenuity of a young Canadian officer, Captain Tony Kingsmill, and a massive artillery barrage along the front, it was the Canadians who succeeded in opening a breach in the Gustav line. Allied troops then advanced across the Liri valley in full force. Despite the beginning of the German retreat on May 12, more hard clashes were necessary on difficult terrain before, on the morning of May 18, the British and Polish forces managed to take the ruins of Cassino and of the abbey respectively. The next objective was the formidable Hitler Line a few miles further north. The 1st Canadian Division was tasked with breaking through the massive fortifications of this second defensive line on May 23. Heavy gunfire and artillery inflicted great damage on the Canadian Infantry and New Zealand tanks who advanced in close range to the guns. The Canadians ultimately penetrated the Hitler Line, liberating the town of Pontecorvo, but with heavy losses. While the British forces advanced in a north-westerly direction, the Canadians proceeded in parallel, with the British to the south and the Liri and Sacco Rivers bordering the other side.

The 5th Canadian Armoured Division played a particularly important role in the advance to Rome, securing a bridgehead at the Melfa River on May 24 and liberating all the small towns en route, including Ceprano, where the Perth Regiment arrived at a meeting point with the British on May 28. In the final days of May 1944, the 8th Army began its attack against the last German defensive line, the Caesar Line, which was the last obstacle on the way to Rome. On May 31 the Canadians occupied the liberated town of Frosinone. While the US and French forces advanced on Rome, the Canadian forces advanced in parallel until they reached the area of Anagni, where on June 4, they were put into reserve.

It was in these final days of May and first days of June that in this area, this theatre of furious fighting, death, and desperation, that one of the most beautiful stories of these years began. It is the story of Gino.

A Working Day Like Any Other

Many D-Day Dodgers, that is — we Canadians who had spent two years driving Hitler's Hooligans out of Sicily and Italy before D-Day — remember those mud slogging days with many mixed emotions. The constant danger from shell and mortar fire whistling at us out of the darkness or the sudden blast of land mines shattering wheels, tracks, or feet, was occasionally relaxed when we encountered Italian civilians trying to return home after the devastating fighting had swept through their area. Their homes had been occupied by the retreating Germans. Our artillery had to lay down barrages of precision shell fire ahead of us as we advanced, so these people sought shelter in the mountains or surrounding remote regions.

Paul Hagen was a young soldier of twenty-one years of age. In 1942, he put on a Canadian uniform for the first time. He was in the 5th Armoured Division and was a driver of vehicles carrying supplies, weapons, fuel, and food for front line troops, as well as evacuating the wounded.

Reinforcements had to be brought in, and wounded had to be brought out so we had to maintain a massive continuous supply line of transport vehicles and all traffic had to move under cover of darkness to avoid the watchful eyes of enemy observation sites and planes."

Trucks were loaded during daylight hours at supply depots a few miles behind the lines. When darkness fell, a well-spaced convoy was formed to move up to the front on mine swept, makeshift roads between white ribbons laid by our engineers.

We would stop a short distance from the front line and, to avoid the loss of massed vehicles, we would send in one vehicle at a time to

3

Army Supply vehicles on their way to the front, packed along a track that the Engineers ran through the Rapido River flats at the junction of the Rapido and Liri Rivers, near Cassino, Italy. 21 May 1944. (LAC, PA 151180)

> *quickly off-load and get back out of there. Coming out we drove past our waiting convoy to stop down the lines to await the other trucks as they came out.*

These excerpts from Paul's memoirs refer to the beginning of June 1944. The American troops had already occupied Rome, chasing the Germans as they retreated northwards following the hard-fought breakthrough of the Gustav and Hitler Lines.

The 5th Canadian Armoured Division, which was part of the 8th Army, was deployed in the south of Lazio, in the heart of Ciociaria, in the province of Frosinone. The war brought Paul Hagen overseas, to Italy, to face the dramatic realities which the bombings, reprisals and fear had created.

There was a continuous flow of traffic from base camp near the Melfa River, between Cassino and Frosinone, to the front line. One warm June evening, Paul was sitting at the wheel of his truck, with Ike Klessen as spare driver, as they were driving back to Cassino after delivering a load of ammunition to the front line. Everything was done quickly, including their drive back towards the pre-selected rendezvous spot which was beside a small gravel quarry.

"A towering horseshoe-shaped area," said Paul, *"which had been carved into the side of a gravel ridge."*

Paul and Ike felt that it would be safe to light a small fire in the shelter of the high bank under a slight overhang. A cup of tea would moisten their dry mouths. They carefully chose a spot out of sight of observers and snipers. They always carried a boiling can, a jerry can of water, packaged tea, and spare jerry cans of gas with them. They laid one of the spare cans of gas on its side, poked three holes in it with their digging pick and made a stove.

Suddenly, in the silence which was interrupted only by the crackling of the fire, they heard a whining sound. They thought it was an animal. *"We could hear something moving in the darkness,"* Paul remembers. They felt worried and their hearts started to beat faster. Now they were frightened. They thought for a moment of their Sten guns which they had left on their truck, but the truck was parked too far away for them to be able to get to it quickly.

"I was sure it must be an animal looking at us over the rim of an excavation about ten feet away. Wild animals would not have come that close to humans," he tells, *"and it was not growling. It must be a dog."*

They were reassured when it started to bark again, even if they still had some doubt. They decided to check and move towards the spot where the yips were coming from. It was a dark corner, far from the glow of the fire. Paul and Ike stared into the darkness searching for something, and at a certain point they saw what they thought was an animal.

"When the animal rose on its hind legs," Paul remembers, Ike gasped: *"Hey it's a kid!"*

"Aspate, Aspate," Paul said softly in his best Italian.
"Wait. We're Canadians. We're friends."
The child froze, then ran towards him.
"You're not German. You understand Italian?"

THE MEETING

GINO WAS FIVE YEARS OLD and had been wandering around the few houses in a small hamlet in the province of Frosinone for a long time, too long. He had no choice but to look for food like an abandoned animal. He had tried several times to find his mother, but her grief caused by the loss of those she loved, extreme poverty, the war, and suffering had driven her mad. People said that his mother wandered in the woods, howling like a wolf. With her mind full of desperate thoughts, she had begun to drift around the hills following the madness of her ghosts. She moved, slow and circumspect, like a stalked and frightened animal. She spoke to herself, and perhaps remembered that she had a son, little Gino. Maybe, in moments of lucidity, she had even tried to look for him. But Gino's mother's physical and mental wanderings had caused her to lose track of him.

Gino saw his mother in that way, "changed" into a wolf, prisoner of a madness which made it impossible for her to look after either him or herself. Still, when he thinks about it, he cries like only a child with a broken heart can do.

The little one must have followed her for a while as she drifted around, but one day, after wandering off to look for food, he lost her. He shouted and ran in all directions, he prayed, but no one answered. He was alone. To survive, he ate wild plants and sheltered where he could.

He learned to bark and whine, perhaps imitating the sounds his mother made, and to look for any type of food to stop the pangs of hunger. He tried to approach some German soldiers, but they chased him off roughly. He tried again with the English, who took him in briefly and gave him his trousers, which were now worn and dirty.

Many years later, memories of this time came back to Gino which he thought had been lost forever:

I was in the ruins of a house on the slope of a hill and, scared to death. I watched a fight between a German military column and a formation of allied airplanes. The offensive began in the afternoon. The planes attacked the Germans by diving at them, and trying to defend themselves, the Germans fired back at them wildly. After every attack the aircraft flew off, only to come back and attack once more. From up above, I could see everything, the convulsive movements of the vehicles which were trying to avoid the aerial offensive. They zigzagged crazily along the road. Many of them skidded and ended up off the road. Others caught fire... It looked as if it would never end. Finally, the airplanes flew off and did not come back.

Gino had no intention of moving from this house he had found, or at least not for a while. The ruin was his safe place, and there was a pallet to rest on. When the roaring of the airplanes, the shooting and the explosions had stopped, he heard the screaming of the soldiers and the noise of the tanks which were starting to move again. The soldiers who had survived the raid regrouped and then marched off.

Afraid that they might see me, I stopped watching and waited for that hell to end. I had not yet recovered from the fright when it started to rain. I curled up as best I could in the most sheltered corner of the ruin, and waited, all alone, for night to fall. The following morning it was hunger that made me go out. I started to walk around warily, looking for a tuft of an edible plant. I had learned to recognize chicory was good, and I was lucky when I did find a little. I went down the hill towards the road which had been the theatre of the previous day's fighting. A lot of destroyed vehicles were off the road, on my left. I did not see any soldiers. Continuing to walk, I glimpsed in the distance some women and children who were climbing onto and off a trailer which was on its side in a ditch by the road. I started to run to see what was happening. The trailer was loaded with rectangular-shaped loaves. It was white bread, which I had never seen before. What I had managed to eat before had always been dark and round. Much of the load had ended up on the road and absorbed a lot of water, but I managed to find some pieces which were still dry. Finally, I was able to calm the feeling of hunger which was always tormenting me. I ate until I was full, and for that day the problem was solved. I hid the remaining bread in a dry corner of my shelter and went back to wander the countryside again. I went back to the road where I had found the bread to have a better look. For the time being the hunger pangs had gone and I was able to give way to my childish curiosity and forget my fears. I was able to observe what had happened more calmly. I saw a helmet covered in blood and some ripped uniforms with burns on them. I realized that I was not alone and noticed with joy that there were other children there, curious like me. Some of them were in the drivers' seats of jeeps which had been hit by the planes, others were pretending to be soldiers and pretending to fire into the sky. I did not want to play those games, so I just watched. Shortly afterwards, though, the sound of a vehicle in the distance brought everyone back to reality. The games stopped immediately and without hesitating we all ran off in different directions. That evening I went back to my shelter, but when I looked for the piece of bread that I had saved that morning I could not find it. Perhaps an animal had found it and carried it off. It was too late to look for something to eat, I lay down with an empty stomach.

And yet another memory emerges from the fog:

One morning I woke up early and started wandering around, once again driven by the same wearying need to find something to eat. Wandering aimlessly, I found myself close to a German encampment. I noticed some cans thrown in a pile, Warily I went up to the pile, and started to look through it. Finally, I found a round can, larger than the others, with quite a few beans in the bottom of it. I grabbed it and ran off, afraid that someone might shout to me to leave it where it was. I hid and scooping up the contents with my hands I started to swallow them greedily, hardly chewing, until my hunger disappeared again.

After that, I went back to wandering around until it was evening. I did not find anything else. All I could do was drink water from puddles, which I scooped up with my hands. If the water was low, I bent down and lowered my lips to the ground. Then I got strong stomach cramps, perhaps because of eating the beans so greedily, and

*because they were old. I squatted out of the way to relieve myself. The
pains disappeared almost straightaway, but I noticed with surprise
that not everything had been digested. In the feces there were still a
lot of beans. My stomach rumbled continuously. So, with the help of a
stick, I separated out the beans and ate them again.*

Gino found refuge in a gorge, not far from the place which, until recently,
had been his house. The neighbours tried to help him for a while, but the
weight of the war had become unbearable for everyone.

A few days earlier, on May 30, the area had been the theatre of a violent
clash between tanks. The bombing had left holes in the ground, destroyed
houses and wiped out crops. It had caused many deaths and left the survivors
with the echo of explosions and screams. Like an animal driven by instinct,
as an overpowering response to his fear, Gino wandered around not
knowing where to go or what to do other than avoid danger. Full of grazes,
covered in dust and mud, with his stomach seized by panic and hunger, he
found shelter in that gorge which had probably been created by the furious
fighting. And there, with his head in his hands, rolled up in a ball, thinking
of nothing, except what was echoing in his ears, he waited for hell to end.
Time went by, and with the passing of time the sense of panic and terror
also began to melt away. With clothes as threadbare as his soul, he chose
that place to be his home, and tried to survive in the only way he knew,
eating wild plants and fruit. It was there in his refuge, cloaked in darkness,
that he heard those unexpected noises. He heard soft steps, metal, voices,
even though he did not understand the meaning of the words which he
heard. Then the fire, a flash of light in the darkness, which hurt his eyes and
opened an abyss in his heart as he recalled the hot flames which warmed
the kitchen where he and his mother spent most of their time. Suddenly,
the loneliness and tiredness had become too great a weight to bear.

Hope compelled him to spy on the two men who were there in the
light of the flames. He tentatively moved closer. He did not know how to
get their attention, so he decided to yelp. When they heard this, the men
around the fire froze, on their guard. Gino saw them turn toward him and
narrow their eyes to see through the darkness to find out who or what could
have made such a sound.

Then he barked again. He tried to arouse their curiosity. He couldn't remember the last time he ate food, which was worthy of that name, when someone caressed him or when he had last bathed. His previous life, with his mother there to look after him, seemed far away, so very far away, crushed by an arid and obscure reality. He was overcome by a frenzy. In his young soul, which had already been put to such a hard test, new hope was born, the hope that, this time, destiny would not be as cruel as it had been up until now. A man approached and Gino stopped barking and instinctively stood up. He didn't know what to do, whether to run away or to stay. How would this man react? Would he chase him away callously or invite him up to the fire? Gino was frightened and bewildered.

Without warning the shadow suddenly said *"Aspate."* Then again *"Aspate."* Gino was so surprised that he froze. *"Wait. Siami Canadasi. Siami amici,"* he heard it said in strained Italian. *"We're Canadians. We're friends."* His fears dissolved like snow in the sun. That voice had said "friends" with a tone which does not belong to the indifference of the English or the harshness of the Germans, but with a kindness which reassured and gave warmth. And only God knew how much warmth that little man of barely five years of age needed.

Gino moved and almost ran over to the man.

"Tu non sei Tedeschi," he said, *"Tu capire italiano?"*

"You are not German. Do you speak Italian?"

On that warm June evening a miracle happened. The devastation wrought by the war had brought together a child who had been orphaned and left to fend for himself, and two young soldiers who, thousands of miles from home, were risking their lives to fight someone else's war. The little boy was hungry. Paul and Ike had him sit by the fire and fed him their precious Bully Beef and hard tack.

He crammed it into his mouth so fast, that I began to fear for his health. In the firelight I could see the little fellow better and I was amazed to note that his stomach was bloated so badly that he resembled a pear-shaped bowling pin with long bare legs and bare feet. His sole garment was a man's shorts which were so dirty and ragged that we could not identify them with certainty, but he said that they were from the 'Inglesi'. We thought that they must have come from our advance

11

troops either infantry or engineers. When asked, he told us that, since the Germans and villagers had fled, he had been wandering around in the mountains eating only grass.

His name was Gino Bragalia and he was five years old. The rest of his story came out in short statements in response to questions from many of my platoon who were joining us around the fire as they completed their run to the front. His father had been in the Italian Army and had been killed in the war. He had no siblings. Talking about his mother made him cry. I was not sure that I accurately understood him because I heard him saying 'She is a wolf', and he kept half sobbing and saying 'Pazzo' which means crazy.

War does not make concessions when something like this happens. The vehicles had to be driven back to the camp before much longer. The soldiers had to decide, and they had to make it immediately.

When our Officer and NCOs drove by without stopping we knew that we had to get back to the camp. Some of the boys left thinking that this was just another war time tragedy. Four or five of us lingered and discussed our limited options. We decided that we couldn't leave him there in the dark in the middle of the night.

So, with Ike driving the truck and little bloated-tummy Gino sound asleep, curled up trustingly on Paul's lap in the spare driving seat, they brought up the rear of the convoy traveling in complete silence back to camp. Gino remembers:

I don't remember exactly everything that they said to me and what I said back, but I felt that I'd finally found some people who I could trust. They welcomed me with great kindness, they fed me with food that I'd never tasted before and which I devoured. I remember very well the moment when they wrapped me in a blanket and put me up in their truck. I fell asleep exhausted, but with every bump I woke up with a start, frightened. The fear disappeared straightaway, however, thanks to the hugs which the two angels gave me. Before I fell back to sleep, I looked, fascinated, at the truck dashboard, all lit up by fluorescent numbers and pointers. Since then, I've always been fascinated by illuminated dashboards, and when I drive at night, I relive those moments.

That night, Ike and Paul had a little well-fed Italian waif tucked snugly in between them. The poor little fellow was so close to exhaustion that he slept like a top with only a few barks and the odd yelp that revealed his troubled dreams.

Morning brought a bright and happy Gino to the lineup forming in front of the cookhouse lorry, boldly holding out Paul's spare mess tin. The old cook was surprised at nothing, but they did get a rise out of him when they told him that McKenzie King was running out of draftees at home and was sending anything he could get, including children like Gino. The cook, who had seen it all in his time, pretended to believe it.

Morning also brought on the problem of finding a way to ensure that their act had not been illegal or in any way could be construed as child abduction. First the news had to be brought to their Platoon Officer. Lieutenant Smith was a real soldier and a genuine gentleman. He was every bit as taken with the young lad as his men were and immediately took charge of the situation. Armed with all the information that Paul and Ike had gleaned from Gino himself and knowing the location where they had found him, Lt. Smith took two of their number who could be spared from that day's run and took off for Gino's home village.

Paul remembers:

They located several people who knew Gino and were aware that he was out there. No one had been able to go out looking for him as there was no transportation left in the village. He had no relatives and there was no one who would have had any way of feeding him if they had found him. Most villagers were destitute and had to rebuild the homes that the Germans and our own artillery had left in shambles.

One of the men with Lt. Smith on the reconnaissance patrol was Lloyd Oliver, known as 'Red', from Miniota. Red was a very level-headed Manitoba farmer with a genius for organizing and managing things, all things. He located an elderly woman in the village who had been a neighbour to the Brigalia family for years. She gave the group the full story. She told them about the decline of Gino's family up until the most recent events: the nervous breakdown of the little one's mother, the disappearance of both in

13

the hills around the hamlet and the inability of the whole community to help them, because of the precarious conditions caused by the war.

Gino really was all alone and had been for weeks or months. It was impossible for the Canadians to establish the length of time with any certainty.

But things were about to change. The Canadian soldiers had been away from their families for a long time, and so understood, at least partly, what the little child was going through. He was lost, left to face the fear caused by the awful things which he had witnessed and by the fight for survival. Life was putting him to the test too soon. How could they possibly deny him help, warmth and affection?

Many years later in a letter to Gino, Paul Hagen remembers:

Those were happy days and sad days all mixed together and very confusing for you as a five-year-old boy as well as for me as I was only a nineteen-year-old boy myself at the time. I came from a large family of seven boys and four girls, and I had been at home among my many brothers and sisters or working for neighbours close to home until the war came along in 1939.

At the time we found you, Gino, I had not seen my family for more than two years and I missed them very much. My youngest brother was not much older than you were at that time, so when I looked at you out there, all alone on that cold night, with your little hungry body all bloated and almost naked and your big eyes shining with fear each time a big German artillery gun fired and the screaming shell passed over our heads you would duck down and cringe close to the ground and I could see you bravely holding back your tears, I thought of my own little brother and how it would be if this war was going on in my country.

At the Camp

LLOYD OLIVER TELLS US:

The boys who had picked up Gino, had by now looked after him for a few days. I had met Gino and like everyone else enjoyed his company. As men far from home and family, it was a novelty to have a small child around.

It seemed to me that a boy of five years of age should have a bath, so I gave him one. His clothes were just what we could find. After the bath, the fellows that had kept Gino must have been impressed, as they asked me if I wanted to look after him. I guess they realized that I truly cared about this malnourished little fellow. So, from that time on, Gino came with me. It was Gino and Red.

Meeting the Canadian soldiers enabled Gino to put the frightening and tense experiences of recent months to the back of his mind and opened a new chapter in the story of his life. It would last several months, during which Gino was transformed and started to live again.

Doug Walker, a driver in the same platoon as Red and Paul, wrote in a letter to his fiancée Mary, on June 12, 1944:

Just returned from a two-day trip and found Gino not far from Rome. He's about 5 years old – without clothes. His family were believed dead. No home, lack of food. His tummy was bloated. Got his permission to take him along. He was all for it. Gave him what they had to eat. Sandwiches and hot tea. It was the first hot nutrition in some time. Now June 12 he is all checked out in pants, shirt and sandals. Eating

Gino with Red and Mert, soon after his arrival at the camp.

with the boys, really in heaven.
*   They are teaching Gino to play ball and all sorts of other things.*
He is a grand little fellow.

The summer of 1944 was hot. The tents hardly screened out the heat of the sun and the invading mosquitoes. Life at the camp was the same, every day. Everyone had a job to do and did it amid the dust, thoughts, tiredness, and tension.

Gino's dreams, initially nightmares, became less frequent and less intense. Little by little, life in the camp became his normal life, and the memory of what had happened before faded away. The rituals, which characterized and organized military life, creating a fictitious stability on the weak foundations of war, calmed that sense of uncertainty which would accompany Gino throughout his life until the discovery of his origins. But this was not the time to think of the future. The soldiers helped him, allowing him to completely become involved in life in the camp, giving him a feeling of belonging. He no longer had his home, he no longer had his mother, but he did have this improvised family just as affectionate and ready to embrace him.

In Gino the soldiers could see their little brothers and sons, who they had been forced to leave behind and who they had not seen for many months. They needed his childishness just as much as Gino needed the security which they gave to him.

In order to access all the services which were available in camp, including meals and supplies, Gino was enrolled first as a private and then as a corporal. His name, Gino Brigalia, which he had given to the soldiers, appeared on the platoon's personnel rosters. He now wore a regular uniform showing his rank. It was someone's spare uniform which had been speedily taken to a local seamstress and altered to be an exact duplicate of the Canadian army battle dress. It fit Gino to a tee.

The soldiers provided him with so many clothes that by the end of his first week in the camp Gino had an ammo box full of them. This was his first piece of baggage. And together with the clothes, arrived shoes, brought up from the headquarters of the Canadian troops in Naples.

Red Oliver and Mert Massey took Gino to live in their tent which was larger than Hagen and Klessen's. Massey was the platoon mechanic. He stayed in his workshop and had a bit more time than the regular drivers, who had to travel almost daily, so he became Gino's daytime tutor and mentor. The rigour with which he taught Gino to count and speak English was at odds with his infinitely kind nature, which was evident in his many poems, one of which he dedicated to his Little Soldier Boy.

The lid of the toolbox which was on the side of the truck was turned into a blackboard where Gino practised writing numbers up to twenty and the alphabet. Red said that Gino learned them all by heart.

Life as a stray had exposed Gino to realities which belonged to a more adult dimension, from which he had absorbed some unpleasant habits such as smoking. Gino smoked even though he still used a potty, from which he could not be parted. And he was equally attached to his blankets and the box of clothes, which he needed with him every time Red left him with somebody else.

Lloyd Oliver explained:

We were young men far from home and family and we enjoyed having a small child around. We would sit in the evenings having a cup of tea, and maybe a smoke or two and a chat. Gino would have a smoke too and tell us a story of when he travelled with the 'Tedeski', the German

OUR LITTLE SOLDIER BOY

He might be just and Itie
In his little khaki pants,
But he might be someone someday
If he only gets a chance.

He has had his share of sorrow.
Seen so much of this old war.
His mother is demented,
While his father is no more.

Life to him is just a puzzle
In which so much mystery lies
You can see so many questions
In his wistful eyes

Tho' we found him in a shell hole,
Nothing on him but a smile,
We all hope someday our Gino
May be someone quite worth while

What a lot of sights and travels
For a boy of just five years.
What a lot of fun and laughter,
And of course, some childish tears

What a lot of boys' attention.
He's our mascot pride and joy.
And we'd sooner lose our pay book,
Than our little soldier boy.

So, when this show is over,
And Adolph is out for good,
Then Gino's going to Canada,
And do what children should.

He might be sort of lonesome
With no sisters or brothers
But he'll always have his soldier friends
His foster dads and mothers.

Merton H. Massey
Miniota Herald, Miniota, Manitoba

soldiers, from Cassino to Rome. We all believed him, but repeatedly told him: 'Don't smoke. You are only five years old!'

In a letter to Mary dated July 3, 1944 Doug Walker wrote:

Gino was beginning to use some English phrases such as 'Take it easy', 'Oh dear' and 'Swinging with you fellows.'

Gino moved around with the soldiers. Red and Mert were the only ones who looked after him all the time, and the little one also followed Red on his night trips, during which he slept behind the seat on a folded blanket. It was during one of these trips, to deliver supplies, that the truck entered a valley. Red describes that:

All of a sudden German airplanes came flying at us. It was quite dark, so their falling bombs made quite a noise. Gino woke up, just as I passed a blown-up bridge. There had been a guard on the bridge, so no one would drive over it. Gino saw the guard jump off the bridge approach and yelled, 'Perkay jump?'. Then, as we drove through the river, he said: 'Perkay aqua?' Everything was 'Perkay?' meaning 'Why?' There is no simple answer to any of these questions during a war.

News spread that in the Canadian camp there was a little soldier of five years of age with the rank of corporal, that he spoke English and carried a six-shooter pistol to complete his outfit. Besides the many Italian civilians who were intrigued by this English-speaking child soldier, members of the British, American, other Canadian forces, some of the Polish Army personnel, and even one of the Gurkas who fought alongside them, all dropped by to see the little five-year-old corporal.

Pictures of little Corporal Gino appeared in the army newspaper and even in some papers back home. Paul Hagen wrote:

A lesser personality would have been spoiled rotten, but Gino remained the respectful young boy that we all loved, though a very lively rascal.

Gino remembers that:

In the camp, I was everybody's amusement and company. All of them enjoyed having me around and playing pranks on me, some of which were quite harsh. When Red went away for work, I stayed in the workshop with Mert and George Pittendriegh, platoon mechanics who, to keep me busy and fill up my days, gave me some little jobs, which I did with great care. Whenever I did not have any jobs to do in the workshop, I would ask their permission and go about from one tent to another, always with my big belt and revolver, as they had taught me to do. I knew everyone in the platoon, and although they often played pranks on me, I did not resent any of them. But, when the opportunity arose, I paid them back. One day I saw Vic Worley, one of the biggest pranksters of them all, who was shaving in front of a mirror which was hanging from a nail. He was so concentrated on the task in

Gino in uniform with his six-shooter pistol to complete the outfit.

hand that he did not realize that I was there behind him. I watched him wondering what I could do, and then, when nothing came to mind, I simply yelled at the top of my voice: 'Boom!' I ran off in the direction of the workshop. Vic was so absorbed in his shaving that he jumped and cut his neck. Once he had gathered his wits, he tried to catch me, but it was too late. I had already found another soldier who was willing to defend me.

Red and Mert taught him to say his prayers at night and to keep up regular hygiene habits. At the end of every day Red asked Gino to report what he had been doing, and if something seemed wrong, he did not hesitate to punish him. Because of their duties, the Canadians could not follow him all the time, so Gino was free to do whatever he wanted between one little job and another. The evening, though, was when he had to give an account of his day, which sometimes he looked forward to and other times he feared. He feared possible punishment but looked forward to receiving the affection that bonded him and Red together. Red was a man of few words. If he thought it necessary, he took down Gino's trousers before he got into bed and, without saying a thing, put him across his knees and smacked him. The severity of the punishment was proportionate to the seriousness of the misdemeanour.

One of the heaviest punishments followed a glance that Gino gave under a lady's skirt. The shared comradely environment, together with his natural liveliness, had piqued the child's interest in a lady's skirt and for what he might see under it. He received so many smacks that time, and his buttocks were so sore, that the punishment was as unforgettable as the model and colour of the knickers which Gino had managed to glimpse.

I don't know how often we were called for an inspection, but, when it happened, the assembly was sounded, and we all had to line up outside with tidy uniforms and weapons. I was between Red and Mert with my revolver. On one occasion, it was Major Ekhart, our C.O., who was reviewing us. When he arrived in front of me, he asked authoritatively if he could check my pistol, which was almost bigger than me and could not be fired as it was a dummy, war surplus, which did not work, and which one of the boys had found for me. I handed it to him, and after inspecting it carefully he said that it needed cleaning and lubricating. He told me to make sure that it was clean at the next assembly. We

HE'S CPL. GINO NOW

Manitoba Soldiers Adopt Italian
Waif Found Lying in Shell Hole

By TED SCHRADER

BERT MASSEY

This is the story of Gino Bro-gaia, a little Italian boy who was found in a shell hole by two Canadian soldies. His father had been killed. His mother was in a mental hospital. So this five-year-old bambino was adopted by the two Canadians who found him.

It was the early part of last June. Mert Massey, of Ninette, Man., and Lloyd Oliver, of Minicota, Man., were returning from an assignment. They noticed the child in the shell hole, wearing nothing but a smile. It was obvious he had been abandoned, so they took him with them.

From his first photos, it was plain that he had suffered from the ravages of war. Deprived of food, clothing and shelter, driven from one place to the next, he lived as in a nightmare.

But this little lad has recovered from his bad dreams. Care and affection have been lavished on him by his foster parents. He is developing into a strong, husky lad

The Canadians are teaching him English, and he is mastering the strange, new tongue. They have taught him to say his prayers. He has a Canadian primary reader and stories of the Bible.

Gino learned his prayers were effective. A camp dog became owner of two puppies. This pleased Gino, but he wanted more. He was told if he prayed he might get his wish. So the prayers were said, at first without avail. They were said again and again. Soon two more puppies showed up.

The little Italian was supplied with a uniform, and taught respect for the officers. Recently Gino was promoted from private to corporal.

Gino travels everywhere with the 5th Canadian Armored Division, and some day hopes to accompany them back to Canada. His foster parents hope he will, too.

Lloyd Oliver and Adopted
Gino Brogalia

The Winnipeg Evening Tribune, 8 February 1945.

22

broke ranks and I looked at Red, who gave me a look which meant that I must follow orders. So, I went off to the workshop and started cleaning. A few days later there was another call for an inspection. I noted that there weren't many of us there. I didn't hear the blast of the trumpet, but an order was an order, so I got into line in my usual place. Strangely, I was the only one who was armed. I was sure that I had cleaned and oiled my weapon perfectly, but to my great surprise Major Ekhart berated me again. I took it badly. I heard muffled laughter but standing to attention I couldn't see who it was. When the inspection was over, I spoke to Red, and, smiling, he answered that orders were orders and that he couldn't do anything about it. I went back to the workshop, took apart the revolver, and began rubbing it again with a clean cloth, sure that I would pass the next inspection. As usual, I went back to biking around the camp and playing with various boys in the platoon or spending time in the workshop with Mert and George. Several days went by, and then one evening Red informed me that the following day there would be another inspection. Once again, I checked that everything was in order. The following morning, I went to get into line. Just like the previous time, there weren't many of us there, there was no trumpet blast, and something new and strange, there was a major who I hadn't seen before. When it was my turn, I handed over the pistol and was admonished again. This was the limit! To make matters worse, my friends were sniggering. It had become my cross. I was tired of being reprimanded always for the same reason. Not long after that it was the same thing again. This time, though, taking advantage of Red's absence for work, I took his revolver - the real one - which he carefully hung in his belt in a corner of the tent, and put it in my holster. The following morning there was a good group of us, all in line with our weapons. Everyone had a gun except me. Reviewing us once more was Major Ekhart. When he arrived in front of me, he asked for the revolver. I tried to take it out of the holster, but it wasn't easy, so Ekhart helped me to take it out. Once the Major had the pistol in his hands, he realized that it wasn't the usual dummy. He turned pale, looked hard at Red, and speaking to me, berated me sternly, saying that revolvers shouldn't be kept in holsters with the safety catch off.

At the end of review, he went to Lloyd. I saw him talking at *length with the Major. Immediately after that, Red called me, and we went into the tent together. He bent over, opened the holster, took out the revolver and put it back into his own holster. He gave me back my old pistol and told me to go outside and play. That evening, as usual, before I went to bed, he had me say my prayers, but wouldn't let me go straight to bed. He wanted to talk again about what had happened at the inspection. He scolded me harshly for exchanging my pistol with his, lay me across his lap and gave me a good spanking. The following day my buttocks were still sore. While I was getting dressed, I picked up my white belt, and saw that the holster and pistol had disappeared. They were gone forever, and that also meant that there were no more inspections.*

Doug Walker writes in a letter to his fiancée Mary, dated July 20, 1944:

The little rascal is coming along famously. Did I tell you he got scissors the other day and went and cut great chunks out of his hair. Typical 5-year-old. He is certainly growing fast. He has more clothes than I have now. It will be a sorry day when he leaves us!

Amused, Red told of another episode in which Gino showed a great sense of initiative:

Another time, I had a boil on my knee, so I couldn't go to work. Gino and I took the opportunity to sleep in. When we later woke up, the kitchen was closed, and I said to Gino: 'I sure would like something to eat.' So, off he went to return with two sandwiches. I inquired to where he had got them, and I learnt that Sgt. Major was having breakfast, and I guess Gino figured he didn't need sandwiches too.

To make the heat of that long summer a little more bearable, one day when the sun was beating down oppressively on the camp, Red got a shovel to dig a hole. He intended to line the base of it with his gas-mask cape and make a sort of little pool. For Gino the sight of Red digging a hole was traumatic. A sudden, undecipherable feeling made his knees buckle and a pain spread-out from his stomach. It was an irrational but strong feeling linked to images which were hidden in the depths of his mind. Gino ran off. He went down the line of trucks and from behind a big truck tire he spied on Red who understood that his attempt to make that hot day more pleasant had had the opposite effect, stirring up the memory of who knows what traumas. Red decided, however, to carry on with his work, hoping that Gino would realize what he was doing. He dug the hole, lined it with the cape and filled it with water, all the time watched by Gino. Then he took off his boots and socks, put his feet in the water and started splashing. Red's face expressed a sensation of deep happiness, and

Gino, on his bicycle, next to Red.

Gino, seeing this unexpected development, moved nearer, a little wary to start with, but then increasingly confident. He was happy that those awful thoughts which had crossed his mind just minutes before had now gone back into the dark place where he had relegated them.

Red wrote many years that later:

> *I guess he had seen so many men buried in a shallow hole, that he wasn't taking any chances. But, from that day on he always wanted a 'wee bird bath.'*

The soldiers constantly thought and worried about that little five-year-old orphan. So a bicycle appeared, found who knows where by the soldiers, so that Gino could have fun cycling around the camp. The little corporal, sitting astride his bicycle in the photo with Red, became the camp's messenger boy and learned to ride even with just one hand. Someone else gave him a pedal car, it was a small jeep which was then painted with the company's insignia and given a corresponding registration number. These details made it in all respects a vehicle of the Canadian expeditionary force. As such, it could be regularly serviced in the workshop and Gino effectively became a driver, like all his colleagues.

Gino remembers:

I remember that I had stopped wearing my summer uniform because Fall had begun, and it was then that I was given a fantastic little pedal car. It was the best present I ever had, and, with the captain's permission, the boys had registered it as a regimental motor vehicle.

Then, once again, on August 25 Doug wrote to Mary:

Our Gino is sweet. He has his showers with us and everything. They built him a nice airplane and painted it blue and white. If the future is not kind to him, he is certainly having the time of his young life now.

Moving Off

IN EARLY AUGUST A DECEPTION SCHEME WAS ORDERED.
A secret movement plan. All soldiers and officers were to take their badges
off their uniforms and paint out all insignia on their vehicles and tanks.
When they moved out, they had to do so with utmost secrecy. Speaking
to civilians was forbidden, as was dropping chocolate wrappers, empty
cigarette packets, and cigarette butts. Following these rules, the long column
of Canadian troops, vehicles, and tanks moved from the place where Gino
had been found to continue pushing the Germans north. They first arrived
at Lake Bolsena, then at Lake Trasimeno. They proceeded towards the
Adriatic, through Foligno and then Fabriano, often at great peril in the
cover of complete darkness on narrow and winding mountain roads. They
stopped at Jesi to prepare for the attack on the Gothic Line.

It was a non-stop succession of moves and new camps. Gino always
moved with his Unit. In "The Story of Gino Farnetti," Red remembers
some of the journeys he made with the boy:

> One I remember, was when we were moving out one evening. We
> got to the road that was to be our place for the night and we didn't
> have tarps on the trucks. We covered our bedrolls with old truck tarps,
> which served to keep them dry.
>
> Another night, we were loaded up with ammunition and before
> we headed out the officer got us all together to tell us where we were
> going. Our spot that night was up under the big 5.5 guns. We were
> told not to nose around, as everything was booby-trapped. Our
> instructions were basically 'not to enter any houses or buildings at all.'
> So off we went and came into this small town. It was a town like our

rural towns back home, with streets, back lanes, gardens, etc. So we drove down the back lane and got a spot to park. We didn't have tarps on the trucks and no tents either.

So, we put our bed under the olive trees and put our mosquito nets over us and went to bed. Towards mid-night a storm came up and the rain started to pour down on us. Gino crawled into my bed, as the big guns fired away. It was a really poor night as the lightning flashed, guns fired and we attempted to sleep in the elements. I looked longingly over at the house, recalling our strict instructions not to enter it, and continued to sleep on the ground. In the morning we had breakfast and, as instructed, loaded up.

John Basket, our cook had set up his stove in the middle of the garden, which was now on very, very soft ground. John had just got the Dutch oven made and was known to make excellent shepherd's pie. This consisted of dehydrated mutton from Australia, dehydrated potatoes and a pastry crust, and a couple gallons of water. This was dinner or supper. Anyways, I was trying to get my truck to the lane, but when backing up, I ran over John's oil stove and Dutch oven. They were beyond repair, and it put a stop to

Gino in his winter uniform.

28

shepherd's pie.

We were now lined up and ready to pull out. We noticed that the Italian people were starting to come back home after being off in the hills, away from fighting. This young boy was running towards his house, the one we had been looking at all night. He ran in the front door, but a loud bang sounded, and the next thing I saw was his mother holding his foot with a boot still on it. This was what remained of her beloved son.

This hard life's lesson taught me: always obey orders.

In the first half of October, after many weeks of intense and bloody fighting, which led to the breakthrough of the Gothic Line, the Division was moved into reserve in the Rimini-Riccione area. The soldiers rested both physically and mentally and got their strength back. The army made recreation areas available which were managed by the Salvation Army. They put on shows and organized sports competitions.

During this time, Lloyd mentioned Gino to his family in a letter dated October 17; Gino often went to Mert's tent on his bike to say hello.

Just now Gino is showing one of the boys how he can count. There will soon be no end to the numbers. Also, the alphabet and prayers.

Just like the other soldiers, Gino was totally involved in military life. He went to watch the shows of the Canadian Women's Army Corps (CWAC), a non-combatant branch of the army which was established on August 13, 1941 in response to personnel shortages. As women were not allowed to fight, they worked as secretaries, clerks, canteen staff, drivers, and occasionally organized song and dance shows to relieve the tensions from fighting and of military life in general. The CWAC was abolished in 1946, and years later, in 1964, women would be completely integrated into the Canadian Armed Forces.

On November 20, 1944 Gino went along with the boys to watch one of the performances:

The C.W.A.C. was on. Took Gino along. Lots of laughs." Doug writes, "What a kid! He sure liked Canadian girls. He now wants to know when the war will end, and he can go to Canada. Another chap took

Gino to see all the Canadian nurses at the hospital. Gino was thrilled.

At the time that Gino and his colleagues were in the Rimini area, the headquarters of the Eighth Army were in Cattolica. A unit of the Office of Strategic Services (OSS) was also based there. This special American branch of the Army was formed in 1943, and one of its duties was to gather information behind enemy lines about Nazi positions and strategies. To achieve these objectives the OSS maintained contact with the various European Resistance groups, and in Italy worked very closely with the Organizzazione Resistenza Italiana (ORI). From Cattolica, through the radio station 'Radio Italia Combatte', the OSS broadcasted information and encoded messages to the 'patriots', another word for partisans.

Tony Monti was an Italo-American and was an agent in company A of the OSS. He had been selected to work in Italy because he spoke the language of the country. He too had heard rumours of a little boy living with the Canadian soldiers. Partly to satisfy his own curiosity, but above all to check that the presence of an Italian child amongst the allied troops did not pose a potential threat, Tony decided to visit the camp where Gino was living.

As soon as Tony saw him, he fell in love with the little rascal and spent the whole day with him. He took photographs of him; they toured the camp and had a lot of fun together. Tony could not resist going back to see him a few more times while the Unit was still in the Rimini area.

A few months later these meetings would prove to be decisive and would unexpectedly change the little boy's life.

As fall continued little Gino found a new, occasional playmate. It was a camp dog with two puppies. Gino didn't hide the fact that he was dreaming of more puppies, all for him, and Red advised him to add this wish to the prayers which he said every evening before bed. *"Your prayer might be answered."* So, Gino prayed, but the wish was not granted straightaway. He continued to pray and, lo and behold, three more puppies arrived. As an adult, Gino remembered this episode and wrote a poem from which one intuits that the dog was a metaphor for a certain period in his life.

The weeks went by, and the soldiers rested and trained.

Towards the end of November, the Division advanced north, and at the beginning of December went back into action in the Ravenna area.

OPPOSITE: Gino with Tony Monti.

No Name

A little dog I'm among people
all distracted they pretend nothing's amiss

He sniffs about, watches, searches, and trembles
his life will no longer be serene

Someone notices him, strokes him, takes pity
he hopes against hope, so happy his heart aches

Wags his tail happy and licks the hand
but all of a sudden the hand is withdrawn

Disappointed, he holds out his paw
trembling he waits again for someone to see him

Another considers, would like to intervene
to comfort and alleviate his suffering

But he's just a mongrel, not a hunter
he's good for nothing, he's not a pure breed

He'd give his life for a bit of love
but it's late, he'll no longer have a name.

Gino, March 9, 1993

Gino with the much wished for puppies.

Ravenna was liberated by Canadian units on December 4, 1944. From January 1945 the front would remain at a standstill for the rest of the winter along the line of the Senio River, the so-called "Winter Line."

CHRISTMAS 1944

IN RAVENNA, MERT MASSEY AND EVERYONE from the workshop were billeted in a large house in the town centre, while the drivers stayed in the east of the city and Gino stayed with Red. Although he was thousands of miles away, Gino continued to be the object of affection of the soldiers' families in Canada, who were continuously kept up to date on his progress.

For the soldiers, another Christmas far away from home was tinged with feelings of homesickness and melancholy. Gino, on the other hand, had probably never experienced Christmas as a nice break from the usual and sometimes difficult routine. Certainly, the few resources which he and his mother managed to live on would never have changed at Christmas. For the Canadians, it was a different story. Celebrating Christmas was important to them even if they were far away from their families, living in conditions which were very different from the ones shown on the postcards; scenes of Christmas trees covered in lights, and wrapped presents waiting to be opened. To remember the comforts of home, Christmas dinner was more elaborate and fancier than the usual fare. The Christmas spirit grew, and the soldiers thought back to the last time they spent Christmas with their families. From overseas they received letters and gifts from their wives, parents, brothers, and sisters which helped them to remember and allowed them to feel the intensity of an affection which the great distance could not subdue. In the bustle of Christmas, the families also thought of Gino. He too received letters and gifts and in return sometimes wrote letters of thanks.

"Dear Laura," he wrote to Ernie Kane's wife, *"Thank you very much for the book which I received today when Ernie got his Christmas parcel. It was*

Dear Laura,

Thank you very much for the book which I received today when Ernie got his Xmas parcel.

It was very nice of you to send it, and I hope to see you soon.

Good-bye for now

Love,

Gino Bragalia.

=

Italy,
1944

Dear Folks,

Well this is the second Christmas Greeting Card. But I guess you don't mind. I received a letter from you to-day. Very glad to hear you are all well happy. Everything over here is very wet but still under control. We are still in Billets and sure hope to stay here.

Today I got a parcel from Joan. In it there was a few books for Gino. So now he is busy coloring them. I guess he will have a lot of stuff

when it all gets here. He got a book and a couple of pair of socks from Mert today.

So he is well away now. I just don't know how Mert is now. But I guess as usual he is ok. I'll have to go to see him soon.

Well Father I guess this is all now. I hope it finds you all well & safe. And I hope to God that your Christmas is a very Merry one.

Cheerio for now. Lots of love,

Lloyd (One from Gino X)

very nice of you to send it, and I hope to see you soon. Good-bye for now. Love, Gino Bragalia."

Gino had never written to Santa Claus before. He didn't even know who he was until some of the boys told him about the smiley old man dressed in red, with a moustache and long, white beard, who so generously makes the wishes of children the world over come true. Gino was fascinated by the picture of his sleigh flying through the sky, pulled by reindeer, and loaded with presents. Maybe one of those presents was for him. "But what do you have to do to get it?" Gino kept asking. "Just write a nice, polite letter," they told him, "And Santa is sure to answer."

The letter was sent on Christmas Eve 1944.

"On Christmas Eve Gino was ready to go to bed," writes Lloyd Oliver. *"He had written his letter to Santa asking for a new bicycle, and he had his stocking hung by the fireplace. The fellows who had painted up this old bike, left it behind the porch door till Gino was asleep. When they went downstairs to get Gino's bike it was gone. Somebody had stolen it from behind the door. We had to fill the stocking with candy and socks. But that was fine with Gino, he still had his old bicycle."*

The soldiers, however, didn't want to let Gino down. He had placed so much hope in Santa Claus and in the letter, he'd sent, and they wanted him to have good memories of Christmas.

"Luckily another one of the fellows," remembers Red, *"said there was a small bike at his place. So, he retrieved it, and it proved to be better than the first bike the fellows had painted. Gino was very happy and by the time parcels started to arrive with yet more stuff for him. He got clothes, socks, sweaters, and the bike. So, we had to get him a bigger ammo box to hold it all."*

"I received your parcel," writes Doug, *"and the flashlight was an ideal choice...Gino sends you a big kiss and hug for the jars of sweets. He loves to crunch hard candies – no matter how many times he is told not to, he insists on doing it."*

Another letter dated January 29:

A Christmas Gino will not forget. Took him to the pictures to fill his day out just right besides getting him away from the inebriated fellows.

Even in wartime, far from home, the soldiers' Christmas spirit was strong!

Clouds on the Horizon

FOR MERT, THE BEGINNING OF 1945 was a good moment to write another poem for the little boy.

Everyone was convinced that Gino would stay with them forever. The Canadian soldiers imagined the boy surrounded by the smells and colours of their home country, far over the ocean. Each one of them hoped to be able to take him home at the end of the war. They were kind and thoughtful with him when he was frightened and didn't trust them. They welcomed him into their camp and made him a member of the big, solid family which they had become. They were foreigners, fighting a war which was not theirs, in a country which was not theirs. Gino had touched their hearts with his story and enriched their lives with his cheerfulness, ingenuity, and the great affection which he had for all of them. How could they even vaguely think of parting from him?

Paul wrote many years afterwards:

As we traveled around the province, all the Italian people that we spoke to seemed quite content to see that you were happy and well fed. They all felt that it would be best for you to stay with us when the war ended since we were not able to locate anyone in Frosinone who was of your Mother's or Father's family.

It was not important to know right now who would look after him. This was a decision which could be postponed. Everyone was certain that Gino would follow them wherever they went.

"*I don't think,*" continues Hagen, "*that there was a single soldier who didn't announce that his family was prepared to adopt Gino and it was*

To Gino

A brand-new year has just begun
For you, I hope, a happy one,
And if my wishes all come true
This year holds much in store for you.
I know life puzzles you just now
But keep on asking why and how,
And someday like all clever men,
You'll know how, why, and where and when.
Stick with your counting, ABCs
For sometime you'll be needing these.
And don't forget your prayers at night
Or what happens to boys that fight.
And so my little pride and joy
A happy new year 'soldier boy'.
Each night and day the whole year thro'
I'll hope and wish the best for you.

M Massey

beginning to look like we were going to have to cut cards for him."

As time went by, however, this rock-solid certainty that nothing and nobody would ever be able to separate the young Italian mascot from his Canadian Division started to look a little less certain.

But as Paul wrote:

...as the time passed, we started worrying about the possibility that the Italian Government would object to an Italian child being taken out of the country by foreigners. The new Italian Government was just being formed after Benito Mussolini was deposed so our government wanted to help them take over their country as smoothly as possible and we did not want to give them any reason to resent our forces being there.

The certainties began to crack. Unbeknownst to Gino, his future had become the subject of debate and disagreement. The soldiers felt powerless as it looked more and more unlikely that they would be able to make their dream come true and take Gino back to Canada with them.

It was a difficult time. So far, no one had found the courage to talk with Gino about it. How could he ever understand reasons which were so much bigger than him? How do you tell a child who has already gone through so much that his hopes were about to be crushed due to higher considerations? How do you tell him that there wouldn't be any fatherly spankings from Red, or affectionate scolding from Mert, or counting and reading lessons, or reassuring lines with the mess tin in his hand, or the opportunity to ride around on his bicycle?

Some soldiers, not only from their Unit, but also from others, and even some American soldiers, proposed getting around the difficulties by hiding Gino inside their vehicles until they were on the other side of the Italian border. After that no one would be able to make objections.

At the beginning of February, rumours started to circulate that it was likely the Canadians would soon be on the move again. The front was still in stalemate on the Senio River, so the drivers' work was not too demanding. It was a good time to prepare a nice surprise for their *little soldier boy*. It would be a happy moment which Gino would remember for a long time. Red and his comrades decided to organize a nice birthday party for the little boy. As no one knew when or where he was born, they decided that February 6 would be Gino's sixth birthday. They prepared a real party

41

for him with music, lights and decorations cut out of newspapers. In the kitchen the cook got to work and did his best to make a birthday cake which was beautiful even if it was not exactly what he'd envisioned.

The soldiers put the cake in the middle of a table they had prepared, and then stood around it so that it was hidden from the child's view. When Gino was brought into the beautifully decorated room, he asked, "What's going on?" Then the soldiers slowly moved away, so that he could see the surprise. Gino was delighted, speechless. It was wonderful. He had never seen anything like it before. There were also six lit candles on the cake, and while he was blowing them out everybody sang *Happy Birthday*. The soldiers' laughter was, however, tinged with tears. To round the party off, they had also brought presents: a shirt, socks and some other small gifts.

So much sensitivity and so many kind gestures from the young men that were here in this country to fight!

Canuck Adopts Italian War Orphan

By KATHLEEN ENGLAND

Edmonton, May 21.—In the not-distant future, God willing, there'll be a very gay party at the home of Mr. and Mrs. A. P. Major to celebrate the homecoming of one of their sons, Driver Leslie Major, 5th Canadian Armored Divisional Troops, RCASC, and his 5½-year-old adopted son, "Corporal Jeano," an Italian boy who travelled with Major through two and a half years of fighting in Italy.

Major, who went overseas in 1941, was with the first Allied troops to land in Italy, and that was where he met little "Corporal Jeano," who was orphaned when a bomb struck his home and killed his mother and father and two brothers. Jeano was playing in the yard when the bomb struck, and was the only one of his family to escape death. Terror-stricken, he set off through the woods.

By a miracle he wasn't killed in the days that followed, as there was fierce fighting in that area. Days later, torn and bleeding and filled with fright, little Jeano came into Major's camp.

He was covered with dirt — his boots were so laden with mud that he could barely lift them, and his clothes were torn to shreds. Major is fond of children, and, as he comes from a family of eight, he knew just what to do. He took the little fellow into his tent, took off his muddy boots and clothing, bathed him, and treated the bruises and scratches on his arms and legs. Then he opened a parcel which had come from home—and a little while later Jeano had fallen asleep in an army blanket wrapped round him and a cracker spread evenly with cheese, clutched in his hand.

In the days that followed, Major and Jeano became fast friends, and it was not long before the little boy was speaking English—after two and a half years of travelling and living with the Canadian unit—he remembers only a little Italian, and when he's asked his nationality he maintains stoutly he's a Canadian!

Major, assisted by a couple of cooperative buddies, cut up an old uniform and made a regulation little dress for Jeano. One day they found a couple of corporal's stripes, and promptly Leslie sewed them on. Like most soldiers, Jeano enjoyed leaves—and he got them every time Leslie did. His favorite was their trip to Rome, and he often asked afterward: "Next time we get a leave, can we go back to Rome?"

Last December, Major was wounded and hospitalized. Jeano was inconsolable, and though he realized that most corporals don't cry, he wept quietly for hours. Major's friends tried to comfort him, but, heartbroken, he cried: "Daddy's been wounded and will never come back!"

When Leslie was transferred to the Western Front, he had to leave Jeano with the Red Cross. The boy is now in an institution for orphans, but Major is trying to adopt him legally so that he may bring him home with him when he comes.

Jeano has already heard a lot about his new family—he calls Mr. and Mrs. Major "Grandpa" and "Grandma"; and he also has five "real uncles"—the Major sons, Staff Sgt. Harry, L. Cpl. Eric, Cpl. Allen, and Pte. Howard, all overseas, and young Bernard, 16, who is in the Air Cadets. In each parcel, Mrs. Major used to include a special package for her adopted "grandchild."

Major's mother and father are fervently hoping that Jeano will be given permission to come out here. Though they have already reared eight children of their own, they want to give smiling, black-eyed, Corporal Jeano a chance to grow up in this peaceful Canadian city.

"Corporal Jeano" with Driver Leslie Major of Edmonton.

Canuck Adopts Italian War Orphan. Globe & Mail May 25, 1945

THE FAREWELL

BETWEEN MID-JANUARY AND THE BEGINNING of February 1945, many Canadian regiments left the Senio area and went into reserve. Some were sent to Cattolica, others to Riccione, and others to San Severino Marche or Urbino.

Gino and his friends were billeted in the north of Rimini where the little one had a chance to play with children of his own age, children from families who lived in the neighbourhood. He was happy. He liked to spend time with his peers, who found him fascinating. He wore a uniform, always had chewing gum in his pocket, and spoke English in a vaguely adult manner. Italian, or more accurately, the Ciociaro dialect of his first few years, was now a distant memory. The children kept their distance at first, then moved a little closer like cats, trying to gauge how far they could go. In the end, Gino was a child, one of them, so he became involved in all their games, from hide and seek to marbles to hopscotch.

This pleasant interlude, however, soon came to an end, when the order came to invoke another deception scheme. Once again, the soldiers had to remove their badges, and paint over the insignia on their vehicles. They were to advance with the utmost secrecy.

At 5.00 a.m. on February 15 the reveille sounded and, two hours later, a convoy of ninety-four vehicles started to move in stages towards the Tyrrhenian coast. Only later would they be told where they were going. When they arrived at Livorno, they boarded a boat to join the rest of the Canadian Army, which was fighting on the northwestern front.

Gino sat with the second driver on the back seat of the truck which Red was driving. He was excited at the thought of the new adventures which were awaiting him. On the first night the convoy stopped at Foligno. From there it went on to Pontassieve, passing through Perugia and Arezzo.

That night they were billeted in tents and the YMCA supervisor put on a show for them entitled *Bermuda Mystery*.

The following morning it was cold, but the sun was shining. The trucks got back onto the road in blocks of twenty-five, with twenty minute intervals between each block. They traveled sixty-four miles, and at noon reached their final staging area, Camp Harrod, between Livorno and Pisa.

The soldiers had small tasks to carry out. Some put the baggage in the tents, others did maintenance work on the vehicles, and still others went around the camp looking for old friends and acquaintances who they had not seen for a while. That evening they watched a performance of *City of Conquest,* once again put on by the YMCA. The atmosphere was calm and relaxed.

The following morning, on February 19, there was a Regimental inspection under Company arrangement. All ranks were informed that they were leaving Italy and going to France.

Operation *Goldflake* was the code name for the plan to move I Canadian Corps from Italy to Northwest Europe under the command of the First Canadian Army which would now be fighting for the first time as a unified force on the border between Belgium and Holland.

Before they embarked, the inspections were rigorous. The high command knew very well that during their time in Italy all the units had acquired various types of non-essential and unauthorized equipment and even personnel. Before they left, a determined effort was made to weed out this 'surplus baggage'. One soldier intended to take with him a grand piano, while another didn't want to leave behind the Mercedes he'd found abandoned by the Germans. One armoured regiment tried, without success, to pass off as "command tanks" a certain number of hen-houses full of hens which laid 200 fresh eggs a day.

After their midday meal Red was refueling his truck and Gino was trotting around when Vic Worley shouted out: *"Oliver, I think you have company coming!"*

A high-ranking officer, a colonel, walked up to them.

He inquired whether I in fact was the one who was caring for Gino. I truthfully replied that yes, I was. The officer said that he couldn't come with us, and he would take him back to the D.P. (displaced persons) camp just down the road.

The dreaded moment had arrived without warning, bringing with it dismay and anguish. Red could not agree to it. He couldn't so suddenly pass Gino over to people he didn't know, with no certainties about his future. After several long moments of bewilderment, Red quickly tried to find a solution:

> *I explained, that I wished to take him back to Viserba to someone who knew him. The officer said: 'Ok but take the sergeant with you and come right back.'*

What could he do now? Red's head was spinning. He looked to his comrades for support, and they gathered around him, willing each other to be strong in the face of this critical, painful trial of separation.

Not even the horrors of war had managed to touch the soldiers' hearts as deeply as the prospect of this farewell. Some of them could not hold back the tears as they thought of *their* little boy, of when a few months earlier they'd welcomed him into their camp, of the pranks which had made them so angry, but had also made them smile, of his genuine amazement when he'd discovered something new like Santa Claus, or when he was given a gift. Paul remembered:

> *Seldom have so many war-hardened, callous soldiers felt so strongly emotional over any one little five-year-old orphan waif.*

With a lump in their throats and rising emotion which they could barely contain, the soldiers who had gathered around Red decided to take a collection. They would no longer be there for Gino, but the money which they'd collected would support him, at least materially, for some time to come. This was the only practical thing they could now do. They collected $130 (approximately $7,600 in today's money) which they gave to Red, hardly daring to look him in the face, so he could give it to Gino. It was a considerable sum of money. The daily allowance handed to a Canadian soldier amounted to little more than 80 cents. The remaining pay was sent directly to their families back in Canada where, for example, a newspaper cost 3 cents. The Canadian boys took out their wallets to lighten the load which at that moment was weighing so heavily upon them. They tried to avoid the inquiring eye of the little boy, who felt that the few certainties which he had constructed over the last few months were collapsing.

They didn't know how to tell Gino, how to explain why they had to do it. If they could, they would have always kept him close by, but in the end, they were soldiers and soldiers have to obey orders. Disobeying such an order would mean risking a court martial, and yet the temptation to do just that was great. Some of them thought it, and some said it out loud. But even if they had managed to hide him, then take him away with them, there was a good chance that they would have been discovered. And then they would have had to abandon the little corporal to an even more uncertain fate in a foreign country.

No, taking Gino away was not possible. He would have to understand this, even if no one really had the courage to explain it to him.

It was up to Red to carry out this unpleasant task. He took the boy by the hand and together they walked away from the others and went and sat down behind a tent. With the simplest words that he could find, Red quietly explained that the soldiers had to go and fight in another country and that Gino could not follow them. These were the orders.

Once again that oppressive feeling, a mixture of pain, tears and desperation, came back. Gino wanted to cry, shout, and put up a fight, but although he was a child, during his time with the soldiers he had learned what discipline and obeying orders meant, even when you could not understand the reason for them.

Early in the afternoon, Red, Gino, and Sergeant Les Bryant left the camp in a Jeep, and headed for Rimini. Paul Hagen wrote:

Corporal Gino Brigalia of the Fifth Canadian Armoured Division, Royal Canadian Service Corps was sitting rigidly with tight lips in the front seat.

Gino was silent, his lips tightly closed, with hell in his soul. For him, this separation was yet another trauma. He had no tears to shed, just an immense rage which paralyzed him. He sat like this throughout the drive, without ever looking at Red, who tried repeatedly but without success to cheer him up.

Red drove Gino to Viserba, to number 86 via Cristoforo Colombo, on the road which ran along the town's seafront. This was the house of Cecilia Neri, who he had met when the Platoon was in the area. Lloyd admitted sixty years later:

I have never forgotten the address. We spent several weeks camped at

Viserba. When I was away and was not able to find a place for Gino I would take him to the Neri's house. They had lots of children that he could play with, and I remember that he would tell me about a girl called Cecilia. The Neri family lived about 200 metres from our camp. At bedtime one of the soldiers from our group would go and fetch him if I was away.

Cecilia was one of the Neri family's daughters and it was not easy for Red to convince her parents to agree to look after Gino, at least for a while. He was a boy, he was little, he still acted up, cried during the night, and demanded a lot of attention. What was worse, he did not speak Italian, he was used to being with soldiers and to being independent. The Neris had a large family to look after and worry about, and in those hard times, with little food and money, they couldn't afford to feed another child.

They would have liked to. They did understand the situation, but they could not manage it. So Red started to put to good use the money collected by his comrades, and he gave part of it to the family to pay for both Gino and the family's upkeep. Then he went back to the little one, who, in the meantime, had started playing with the family's children, and, embarrassed, he awkwardly gave him a hug. Gino hardly looked at him. He did not want to get upset.

So, after almost nine months together they parted in silence. At that moment words would have been just useless weights, adding further to what was already a heavy burden to carry.

It was a cold February night when Red and little Gino parted, both with their hearts in tatters. *"A night,"* recalled Red, *"I will never forget."*

Before going back to camp, Red visited the town mayor, who was a representative of the Allied Forces acting as mayor. He was a captain in the English Army. Red gave him the rest of the money and asked him to keep an eye on the little boy. *"He promised me that he would do it."*

Red and Sergeant Les Bryant set off again the following morning after spending the night in a room offered to them by some New Zealand women soldiers during their drive back. They had returned to the rest of the Company by late afternoon.

The lack of time to find an alternative solution, the orders from above which could not be ignored, the traumatic parting, entrusting Gino to the Neri family, Red had done everything he could possibly do to make sure that arrangements for the child were as secure and safe as possible. Despite this, the long days spent in Livorno waiting for the boat to France were agonizing for him. In his heart the Canadian soldier had to abandon his dream of a future back home with Gino and replaced it with bitterness and worry about the little boy's uncertain future.

Red was not the only one who was feeling grief-stricken.

In a letter to Mary dated March 5, Doug wrote:

The saddest news for all of us boys. Gino was held back so the poor fellow returns to his land. We could have gotten away with taking him with us, but someone had to take him for a walk and who should see him but a colonel from brigade. They took him back with them. From what I gather to the town we left and some very nice people who knew him while we were there. Took him with the understanding that the town mayor sees that they send him to school and that the $ 130.00 collected is spent adequately. But even so I can't see the poor little tyke staying around. We all feel so bad about it.

In Livorno, Tony Monti was also following the various phases of the embarkation. He was the Italo-American member of the OSS whom Red and Gino had met in Rimini a few months before, when the Canadian troops were camped there. Monti was in the Tuscan port to carry out his intelligence and to make sure there were not any leaks in the secrecy of the operation.

Red recognized him and stopped him. When he met Monti his separation from Gino was still very fresh. When he closed his eyes, he could still clearly see Gino with an expression of sadness and disappointment on his face. The fortuitous, unexpected meeting with Tony provided him with new hope.

Lloyd was like an overflowing river and poured his anguish onto Tony. He told him about Gino, about the order they had received, and about having to leave him in Italy even though he and his comrades had wanted to take him to Canada at the end of the conflict. Finally, he told him about his decision, approved by the commanders, to drive him to the house of a family they knew rather than to leave him in the refugee camp. Tony listened, nodded, and approved of his decision.

Red gave him a note with the address where Gino could be found, and asked him, if he could, to take the situation into his own hands. Tony reassured him:

"You have my word. I'll look after Gino."

Then the war moved on, and for the Canadians the Italian Campaign was over.

Gino was officially struck off strength that night as we boarded the craft at Leghorn, to catch up with the Canadian Army in France. Our last look at Italy and our new campaign with the rest of our newly battle-scarred Canadian forces who by that time had smashed their way across France and into Belgium.

On February 25, 1945, the day of his twenty-second birthday, Red and his companions left Italy.

At six o'clock that morning, we set sail for Marseille, France. The sea was calm, and I remember being on the deck when we pulled out of port. As Italy faded out of sight, I recall wondering if I would ever see Gino again.

Embarkation in Livorno. With all identification removed, troopers await orders to board their 'Landing Ships, Tank', Leghorn, February-March 1945. (LAC)

NEW HOPE

ONCE ALL THE CANADIAN TROOPS had departed, Tony Monti's mission in Livorno was over and the men from the OSS got ready to go back to headquarters in a villa at Durazzanino, between Ravenna and Forlì. *"You have my word. I'll look after Gino."* The promise which he made to Red continued to echo in Tony's mind. When he arrived in Romagna, he ordered a diversion in the direction of Viserba. He followed the directions which people gave him along the way and, when he arrived at the town, he swiftly drove down the seafront road at the end of which was the Neri house.

The engine of his Jeep was still running when Tony glimpsed Gino playing with the other children. He had grown but still looked like a bit of a rascal, even if he seemed less cheerful than when he saw him in Rimini that first time. The little boy noticed the military vehicle driving up and, with one hand shading his eyes from the sun, he watched it, trying to understand who was on board. When he recognized Tony Monti, he ran up to him, much to the surprise of his playmates. Even though their first meetings were brief, Tony was a link to Gino's friends. Gino ran with the hopes that the man in uniform would tell him there had been a mistake, that the order had been revoked, and that he could go back and hug Red and the others. Maybe he had come for this reason... *"He's here to take me back,"* he told himself again and again as he rushed to meet him. He was so happy as he hoped against hope and ran even faster.

Tony was not expecting such a warm welcome. He saw the little boy flying towards him, and when he got there he heard him ask breathlessly, but in perfect English: *"Are you taking me to Red?"*

He almost felt guilty. "No," he replied. *"That isn't why I'm here. But I do have some good news. You can come away with me if you want."*

Gino thought quickly. It was not exactly what he wanted, but better with Tony than with Cecilia's family. It was true that he was lacking in nothing, but no one around him was wearing a uniform. The relationship was different. He felt like a guest, and often like an outsider. Also, he hardly understood a word they said. His language was English, while the Neri family spoke neither Italian nor his dialect. Both Gino and the family had to use their hands to communicate with each other. This was another reason why he felt like an outsider within the family, and in every situation, so he rebelled in any way he could.

Gino tells us today:

I think I remember Cecilia. Hers is the only female face which I remember from that time. I slept in the same room as her on more than one occasion. I also remember two elderly people, maybe her grandparents. They were there the time when I accidentally cut myself with a knife between my thumb and index finger. I still have the scar. We were in the courtyard. She had long skirts and white hair, he had a beret.

Tony was a soldier. Gino didn't know what he did, but that didn't matter. He spoke English, and, from the way he looked at him, seemed to care about him. That was good enough for Gino.

"Okay, I'll go with you. Where are you taking me?"

They sorted out everything with the Neri family and with the town mayor, and then Tony and Gino got into the Jeep and left for Durazzanino.

Tony was pleased to see that the boy was happy, and at the same time was relieved that he had been able to keep his promise to Red. However, he realized that the problem had not been resolved. In any case, for the time being the little soldier boy would receive the attention and care which he'd grown accustomed to when he was with the Canadians. With Joseph Marcolla, one of his comrades, Monti looked after Gino in the villa at Durazzanino where the American unit was based.

To make his transition from a family to military environment less traumatic, Tony asked a seamstress to alter a small American Army uniform so that Gino could wear it. And he gave him the rank of sergeant. He also asked a shoemaker at the village of Coccolia to alter a pair of army-issue boots so that they could have shoes for Gino. The shoemaker initially tried to change Tony's mind, but then reluctantly agreed to do the work. For

him it was such a waste of a good pair of leather boots. He kept shaking his head: *"I don't understand... what a waste!"*

By now, Gino was accustomed to living with adults, but he was still a child. He was a bit of a rascal, and found it difficult to live with army discipline, even after all this time. A local carpenter had made him a little wheelbarrow, which he pushed around the villa courtyard. He also had a bicycle, the one which was given to him at Christmas in Ravenna. But even though he had so many things, he was not happy about having to follow timetables and rules. He was also the only child at the villa.

Gino recalls:

I remember that at the villa in Durazzanino I used to enjoy sliding down the corridors as if I were ice-skating. The nails in my little boots made them especially suitable for this purpose. Unfortunately, they also made a tremendous amount of noise, and I was often told off for this. One day I ignored a soldier who told me not to disturb him while he was sleeping. He must have been dog tired, but I carried on with my noisy games, until he really got fed up. He got out of bed, started shouting at me and then raised his gun. Fortunately, another soldier intervened and managed to calm him down while I ran off, frightened to death. That was the last time that I went sliding in the corridors.

After various similar episodes, Monti had to accept that the military environment was not the right place for a little boy like Gino, even though he was well looked after there. Gino needed something different. He needed an environment, which was more suitable for a child, the company of friends his own age, the warmth of a family and of a female presence. This became increasingly apparent to the soldiers, so they approached a couple who lived in Coccolia, Antonio Farneti and his fiancée, Rina Zaccaria.

OPPOSITE: Gino and Tony Monti at Durazzanino, where the OSS was based. (Tony Monti)

Antonio and Rina

ANTONIO, WHOSE *NOM DE GUERRE* was Mario Roberti, was a member of the ORI (Italian Resistance Organization), for which he had the task of coordinating the activities of the various units of partisans. They aimed to achieve more solid results in the fight against the Nazis, and at the same time to limit collateral damage in what had become a guerrilla war.

Antonio had grown up in a republican family in the village of Coccolia near Ravenna and was working at the Caproni factory in Forlì when the War broke out. At the factory he started spreading propaganda against the regime, and for this he was arrested and interrogated. He was then called up for active service and sent to the military depot in Venice. Despite being under strict political surveillance, he managed to get back to Ravenna to meet his friends, and together they set up some anti-fascist factions.

He was declared a deserter, and upon his return to Venice was arrested. After the Armistice of September 8, 1943 and the ensuing chaos in the high command, Antonio managed to escape. He went back to Ravenna and, after carefully assessing the situation, decided with a few friends to go south and fight alongside the Allies.

The small group left on bicycles on September 19. They stopped only when necessary, and arrived at Lesina lake, in the Gargano area five days later. After trying without success to contact the Allied commanders, they received permission to carry on to Naples, and there they met Craveri. Raimondo 'Mondo' Craveri, the son-in-law of Benedetto Croce, who was one of the founders of the ORI. He had political and diplomatic acumen and was acquainted with some of the high officers of the Allied command.

The young men were taken to Pozzuoli and trained by the Americans in various disciplines, including self defence, pistol shooting, sabotage and counter-sabotage, printing, spying, using a radio, and receiving drops from airplanes. They then went to Brindisi to learn how to send and read encoded messages. The ORI was founded because of an agreement made with the Americans. The document which they drew up in November 1943 stated that the ORI and the OSS would fight alongside the Allies against Nazi-fascism "with equal dignity."

The ORI guaranteed the supply of intelligence, weapons, ammunition, equipment, and support to all the partisan brigades who were fighting in the north of Italy. When the training was finished, operative groups were formed. Antonio Farneti was mission commander of the *Zella* group, which left from Brindisi on board the submarine *Platino* on the evening of February 16. They headed for Emilia-Romagna and would disembark at the mouth of the Reno River.

This was how Tony Monti and Antonio Farneti met and started working together on intelligence missions. Monti had known Antonio for a while now, knew what he was like and that he could trust him. He had also met his fiancée, Rina, who Peter Tompkins, one of the first members of the OSS, described in his book "L'Altra Resistenza" as *"a girl in her early twenties, slim and fit with bright red hair."* Rina had been a runner for the partisans, and her family had always helped Allied soldiers who were stationed in the Coccolia area, where she lived.

By now Tony had realized that Gino needed to know and experience a civilian lifestyle and spend time with someone who had time for him. He thought highly of Antonio and decided to ask for help. The reply which he received was: *"We'll see what we can do..."*

Rina recalls:

Antonio, who was my fiancé at the time, met Monti when they were working with the OSS, the intelligence service which acted as the link between the Allies and the partisans. I had already been a runner for the partisans while the Germans were here. When the Allies arrived, my mother did their washing, and I did the ironing. Antonio saw Gino at Durazzanino in the villa where he was staying with the Americans. There were not many children in the area who he could play with, and Antonio knew that I was very fond of children, so one day he came to my house with his American friends, Tony Monti and Joseph Marcolla, and said: 'We've brought you our little sergeant!' I was very happy to see that little boy. He was so beautiful...really beautiful. I invited him to eat with us. I used gestures to make myself understood, because Gino only spoke English, very good English. Everything went well during the day. There were many children in the neighbourhood, and they and Gino enjoyed playing together. Gino was always the leader and all the children wanted to play with him. Then evening arrived and it was time to go to bed. That was when the problems started. The little one began to cry and wanted Tony. We spent the whole night trying to calm him down, but to no avail. The following morning I fetched a bicycle, loaded Gino onto it and took him back to Durazzanino. I explained to Tony that the child wanted to be with them, and that I could not keep him with me all night long if he cried for his friends. The Americans knew, however, that their time in Italy was almost up. What is more, they often had to go away to carry out the intelligence and sabotage work...

Every time there was a change in Gino's life, he had nightmares. He had them after meeting Paul and Ike, then again during his first night with the Neri family after parting from Red. They wouldn't leave him in peace, even now in the bed which Rina had given him. So, he cried, was restless, and wanted Tony. He was afraid of being abandoned, even though he really did like being with Rina. He was very fond of her, and she of him. It was too soon to call it love, but it was not far off. A temporary compromise was found:

Thus we agreed that Gino would spend the daytime with me and my family at Coccolia, and then I would take him back to Durazzanino in the evenings, so that he could be with his soldier friends during the night. This system worked. During the day Gino played with all the children from the neighbourhood, had his meals with us, was washed by me and had his clothes, which always had chocolate on them, washed by me. In the evening I would take him back.

Tony Monti's solution, namely taking Gino to Rina in the morning and bringing him back in the evening, was a good one. Gino became accustomed to seeing Rina, grandpa Pippo and grandma Maria, in fact he couldn't manage without seeing them every day. Their house was poor but cosy, and his new playmates were nice. Gradually he learned Italian and the local dialect. He was once more a happy child.

Gino was sound asleep in the villa at Durazzanino when two loving hands wrapped him up in a blanket and carried him off in the middle of the night. It was Tony Monti who, on May 10 at two o'clock in the morning, knocked on Rina's door, and handed him over. He was keeping the promise which he had made to Red soon before he left for Marseille to fight on the western front.

They handed me Geng — I always called him that — then they said to me: 'We're leaving him with you, because we're going home.' After that he stayed with us permanently.

Gino remembers that night very well:

When I was passed over I woke up, but I recognized the voices of Rina and her mother, who were speaking softly, so I wasn't alarmed and carried on happily sleeping.

Just like Red and the many other soldiers who had looked after the child for months, Tony had contemplated taking the boy with him to America, but he could not do it, as Gino had neither documents nor an official identity. Even his age was not certain. In times of war there were no offices which you could go to ask for documentation such as a birth certificate, so the child who was found naked and starving in the hills around Frosinone was simply a statistic of war, just one among many of the war's refugees.

A Family at Last

THE FOLLOWING MORNING, Gino was not very surprised to wake up in a different place with Rina next to him stroking his hair and speaking softly to him. She explained, even if he did not yet understand a great deal of Italian, that Tony had gone away. He had gone back to his home country, across the ocean, with all the others. Tears came to Gino's eyes, so she comforted him and told him that there was no need to worry. From now on she would always be there to look after him.

And so another chapter began for Gino. Left alone by his mother in the middle of a war, then taken in by soldiers who provided him with a safe place to stay and managed to calm the storm of feelings caused by that first intense and terrible abandonment, then once again left with relative strangers, and finally placed in the heart of a new family. Maybe for good. It was difficult to overcome the feeling of precariousness which had been experienced by a child of such a tender age. It was something which weighed heavily on him. Having abandoned the Italian language, he had been expressing himself just in English for several months now, with an additional few crumbs of Ciociaro dialect occasionally thrown in for good measure. Each of these sudden changes had been gut wrenching for Gino's psyche, which he had to reconstruct each time with the limited psychological resources of a five-year-old boy.

Gino was very lucky indeed to be taken in by Antonio, Rina, and their family. Nowadays one might imagine that it was a common occurrence during the chaos of wartime, but in the spring of 1945, it was truly an exceptional act of altruism. Italy was a nation in ruins. Even the most essential things were lacking, and hunger was widespread. Gino was another mouth to feed on an already modest family budget. Worse yet, he did not

Rina happily hugs Gino.

have any personal documents and so was not able to get a ration book. Despite this, Antonio and Rina fell in love with him. They treated him as though he were their first child, even though they were always aware that he could be taken away at any moment by the authorities or by relatives, of whom, however, there was thus far no sign.

It was through this difficult situation that these two young people showed how exceptional they were. Although they were not yet married and had to cope with the prejudices which such a choice could inflame, they chose to ignore the pressure which so many people put on them to place the child in an orphanage. Instead, they did everything they could to find Gino's family for him, so that he could go back to his own people, even if that meant having to lose him.

Rina Farneti recalled:

I received a letter from signora Bianca. I think she was the wife of Colonel Hancock, governor of Milan. In the missive she explained that the Americans couldn't take Gino overseas, as they would have liked, and she heartily advised me to put the child in an institution, close to home so that I would be able to visit him often and follow him as he grew up. Of course, I didn't take any notice of her suggestion. Gino was and would remain with us. Unfortunately, I no longer have that letter. I must have lost it during a house move.

Although he was little, Gino himself remembered his early days with Rina and the family:

I heard various comments. One of them was that nobody knew who my father was, so there was the danger that he might have been a criminal or a good-for-nothing. And if that were the case, I might turn out to be like him, and cause lots of trouble for my new family. Others said that, as I had stumpy hands, I would never grow tall. I would look like a typical "terrone" (southern Italian). Rina and Antonio laughed at this silliness, looked at me lovingly and answered these comments saying that if necessary they would stretch my legs while I slept. I remember one man in particular who would say to me: 'Hello terrone, how are you?' and would then stroke my head. I, of course, did not take it as a compliment!

The idea of adoption, on the other hand, was impracticable. Article 291 of the Italian Civil Code, which was in force at the time, imposed a series of extremely strict rules: adoptions could only take place if the adoptive parents were over the age of fifty, and only if it could be proven that there were no close living relatives. Once more, not knowing about Gino's background meant that another door was closed to him. Gino was invisible, like a Pirandello character.

Rina later explained:

The problems with bureaucracy were enormous. We couldn't adopt him, because we didn't have his birth certificate, and no one knew if he still had living relatives. What is more, we weren't old enough to adopt.

Going to elementary school, which was what all children of his age did, was more complicated for Gino:

There were problems with that, as well. Gino didn't have any documents, and couldn't get any, because we didn't know when and where he was born. He went to school, but his name wasn't written on the register. The fact was, that as far as the authorities were concerned, he didn't exist.

Gino entered the first grade at Coccolia Elementary School. When Rina and Antonio married and moved to Ravenna in 1947, he moved to the Mordani Institute in the town. Neither school, however, were able to give him a report card to take home to his parents. Rina had the unpleasant task of giving Gino yet another explanation in a way that he could understand but that would not upset him too badly.

Mr and Mrs Farneti, however, did not lose heart. They took Gino to a dentist in the hope that by looking at his teeth the dentist would be able to determine his age more accurately.

Gino remembers:

Antonio briefly told him my story, saying that he and mom had adopted me, but didn't know how old I was. He asked if an examination of my teeth might give us some idea. The dentist asked me to open my mouth, and looked at my teeth for a long time. He asked me when I had lost my milk teeth. My dad answered for me, and said that some of them had fallen out in the first months that I was with them. The others had fallen out the following year, so in 1946. I remember it well, because I took some of them out myself with a thin thread and a sudden jolt. The dentist had another look in my mouth, then confidently declared that my year of birth was 1939.

Apart from giving a photograph and written description of the boy to the authorities, Antonio himself went to Rome to ask some regional newspapers to help him trace any possible relatives of Gino's. *Il Rapido* published the photograph and story. It was hoped that someone might recognize the boy and provide information which could be used to reconstruct his identity and trace some of his relatives. It was an arduous task. Italy was on its knees. Few people could afford to buy a newspaper let alone read it with the widespread illiteracy in the country. These efforts did not produce results.

Rina later explained.

All our efforts, the articles which we put in the newspapers and Antonio's trips to the area where Gino was found, didn't help at all.

After reading about it in the press, several people came to our house thinking that because the boy had been left with us by the Americans, he might have a substantial dowery, and they wanted to get their hands on it. Some of them were disgusting.

On February 17, 1946 *Il Rapido*, a Cassino newspaper, reported the following in an article entitled *Possible identification of the blond child living at Coccolia?*:

...As a result of the publication of an article in issue n° 3 of 'Il Rapido', a Mr Filippo Lanciano of Cassino met Mr Farneti. Mr Lanciano told Mr Farneti that he had recognized the child as his nephew! According to him, the boy's father had died tragically during the war and his mother was alive and had been sent to Sicily... Mr Lanciano declared that he had recently returned from a POW camp and was now staying at Torrice (Frosinone).

Gino too remembers people turning up in Ravenna. Some of them claiming to be close relatives:

I was in my dad's store in Ravenna when a man appeared holding a crumpled photograph and newspaper. He spoke very rapidly, saying that he knew me, but my dad wasn't in the least convinced by what he was saying, and neither was I. I did not trust him. He was untidy, with an untidy beard and a shirt which should have been white, but which was white no more. It was yellowish and the collar was dirty. I was afraid of him. He took hold of my hands, turned me round and looked closely at me. Still talking, he then pretended that he had found some distinguishing marks. The thought that I might have to go with him filled me with anguish and then terror. I couldn't wait for him to finish inspecting me, and hoped that he would not take me away, as I had already found a mom and dad. My dad spoke at length. I heard him raise his voice and ask for proof. Fortunately, the man realized that he was not getting anywhere, so walked out of the store and disappeared at the first intersection. For several months after that I was afraid that this awful experience might happen again.

The kindness and generosity of Antonio Farneti and Rina Zaccaria was apparent in the closing paragraphs of an article which appeared on the front page of *Il Rapido* on December 17, 1945. Although *Il Rapido* was the newspaper of Cassino, the entire operation had been forced to move to Rome after the town was razed to the ground during the Allied bombing:

> ... *Antonio Farneti of Coccolia in the province of Ravenna, we, the people of Cassino, survivors of the hurricane, still living in exile without a tomorrow, embrace you and thank you for having welcomed into your home our blond, dark-eyed child. The boy is the son of all of our dead and a symbol of the tragedy which we have experienced, experience now, and will continue to experience.*
>
> *Alcide De Gasperi and Leone Cattani, we the people of Cassino are so weary that we do not even have the strength to curse you. The only ones that we have faith in are the likes of Antonio Farneti, a man from a village called Coccolia which until yesterday we did not even know existed.*
>
> *December 1945*
> *E.A. Grossi*

Although all attempts to have the child recognized by the authorities had failed, life continued happily. Gino was very fond of Antonio, grandpa Pippo and Grandma Maria, but it was Rina that he adored. As an adult, Gino remembered how he felt when he was with her:

> *I remember the deep emotion that I felt when I was in her arms. She transmitted a warmth which I never grew tired of. All the attention, which I had never had before, made me feel protected and wanted. Her smile and her kind face had become fundamental for me.*

Rina, who was a seamstress, made clothes for Gino, bought him sandals, and made sure that her *Geng* wanted for nothing. She surrounded him with all her love and threw herself into the role of his mom.

Antonio and Rina married on June 28, 1947, the day of Rina's twenty-fifth birthday, and Gino was their pageboy. After the wedding, the three of them moved to Ravenna.

Gino remembers:

Gino in civilian clothes at home in Rina's backyard.

Gino at the sea.

When we moved to Ravenna, my parents found an apartment near the rail station. We had been living there for a few weeks when one day mom came up to me and gently held my face in her hands, as if she were going to give me a kiss. She asked: 'Geng, would you like to call me mommy?' It was the best question that I could be asked. I had been waiting for it since the day we first met. Without hesitation I said yes, and we hugged for a long time and exchanged lots of kisses. When I looked at her, she had tears in her eyes... I was surprised. I didn't know that people also cried for joy. I found a handkerchief and dried her tears. Mom stroked my hair and said lots of nice things. I was immensely happy and felt as light as a feather. At that moment I would have done absolutely anything for her. The following day I took a piece of seamstress's chalk and wrote on the wardrobe curtain: 'I love you mommy.' For the rest of her life, even when I was seventy-five, I called her that. It was only when we were with other people that I shortened 'mammina' (mummy) to 'Mina' (also a woman's name), because I was a little embarrassed.

In the meantime, Gino grew and made friends with many children in the neighbourhood. Some of his playmates were the children of fire fighters. They lived at a fire station which was near the Farnetis' house. Whenever he liked, Gino was allowed to go into the station and watch them practice the fire drill. He was fascinated by that environment where discipline, order, skill, and being on the alert were the rule. Maybe it reminded him of the days when he was with the army, even if he was just a mascot.

Gino recalls with pride:

By now at the fire station I was considered one of their children. They didn't take any notice when I went in or out of the building. We were friends. (...)
At holiday time and whenever gifts were distributed amongst the firefighters' children," Gino recalls with pride, "I was the only outsider included in their list.

In the summer of 1949, Rina told Gino that there was going to be a new arrival in the family:

While we were in the dining room, mummy said to me: 'I have news

Geng. You're going to be a big brother. Are you pleased?' 'Yes, I'm pleased,' I answered immediately, and then I gave her a big hug. The following months were calm and happy, with everyone looking forward to the happy event. I often asked questions and talked about the baby with mommy while she prepared the little blankets, sheets, bonnets, diapers, and all of the other things which you need for a newborn baby. In those days these items were made by hand. The most beautiful thing that she made was a little blanket for the pram, consisting of a fine material decorated with lace. During the pregnancy I saw mummy's tummy grow bigger and bigger, and noticed the little troubles which went with it. Every day, after tidying the house, we would take a walk along the road which led to the Teoderico Mausoleum. The road was lined with cypress trees, one row of them on either side, and we would stop every now and then for a rest, while I picked up cones from the ground. At home we often talked about whether the baby would be a boy or a girl, and there was a way of predicting this. Whenever you had chicken, you would pull the wishbone with somebody, and if you were left with the largest part of the bone, it meant that it would be a girl, while the shortest part of the bone meant that it would be a boy. I was always anxious to do this test, because I wanted a little brother, and in fact I was often left with the short piece of bone... One day, not long before the birth, I was doing my homework when mummy asked: 'Geng, what shall we call the baby if it's a boy?' I was so pleased that she had asked me that. I was so excited at the prospect of having a brother and being able to play with him. 'I would call him Max. Do you like that name, mum?' She said that she did. For me 'the maximum' was what I wanted for the baby, and that was why I chose the name 'Max'. On March 9, 1950 the baby was born and that was when I found out that it really was a boy. And a week later Max came home.

When she came home from hospital Rina fed the baby with her own milk, but after a few months she had some problems and was forced to stop breastfeeding and began giving the baby cow's milk instead. Antonio procured an old but reliable bicycle for Gino and gave him the job of fetching the milk. Every evening at sunset Gino jumped on the bicycle and pedalled into the countryside.

I used to go to a farmer who would give me fresh milk. At that time, it was customary to give small babies milk always from the same cow. Sometimes I would have to wait for an hour to have my bottle filled up. It was often quite late when I set off back home, and on the way, I would cycle past some houses with gardens which bordered the road. As it was spring there were a lot of flowers, some of which were growing through the fences. I had an idea: I would surprise mummy. On these trips back I started cutting some of the flowers close to the fence with my penknife and taking them home for her. I decided that it wasn't too naughty, as the flowers were for mummy after all. However, one evening, while I was carefully cutting a beautiful lily, the lady of the house surprised me and gave me a good telling-off. I started to cry and tried to run off, but she was quicker than me and caught me by the arm. She wanted to know who I was and what I was doing there. I told her everything. The lady listened in silence and then, when I finished, said in dialect: 'If only all boys were like that! I'd be happy to have a son like you'. She gave me back the flowers and added some more to the bunch, then with a fond goodbye sent me on my way. The job of 'milkman' lasted more than a year.

Another episode involved a bathing suit which Gino had been asking about for a while. Rina, who worked tirelessly to provide for the needs of the family, had not yet found the time to make one for him, even though she had promised.

My mother was always busy with the housework and her work as a seamstress and had little time for other things. I had asked for the bathing suit so many times that I dared not ask again. Then one day I had an idea. It was the afternoon, and mummy popped out on an errand. While she was away, I took a piece of paper and wrote: 'Mummy, can you make the bathing suit for me, please?' I took the glue which I used for kite-making and stuck the piece of paper to the back of my right hand, and then waited for her to come back. As soon as I heard the house door open, I threw myself onto my bed and pretended to be asleep, but made sure that the hand with the note was well in view. When she came in, she didn't notice anything, and came up to the bed thinking that I was asleep. I heard her read the note, then she kissed my forehead and murmured: 'I'll go and make it for you right away". The following day I wore my new bathing suit for the first time. I was proud of it and enjoyed showing it off on the beach. From then on whenever I wore the suit, I would wash it afterwards with laundry soap and a brush, so all mummy would have to do was iron it.

Antonio Farneti had also been fundamental in Gino's life. Ever since the time when the child spent his days at Rina's little house and his nights with the Americans, Gino had felt esteem and gratitude for the man who would become his father.

I loved my father. He was very good at manual work and taught me how to make toys. When I was still in the care of Tony Monti and the other American boys, I remember that once he put me on one of those motorbikes which were sometimes dropped down on parachutes. They were small and very easy to ride. It was the only time that I did it, but I managed to ride it all right. I felt like a champion until, that is, daddy told me to stop, and I couldn't. He had to run after me and, when he finally caught up with me, to stop the motorbike himself. What a fright we had!

The most personal and perhaps most precious memory which Gino has of Antonio is from their earliest days together, before he was placed in his and Rina's care.

Antonio and a friend of his took me along with them in their truck. We came across a soldier, possibly American or English, lying in the middle of the road. We thought he might be drunk. Because he was blocking our way we couldn't carry on, so Antonio and his friend got off the truck and gently tried to move him but couldn't manage. Then they remembered that I was there and asked me to speak to him in English. I don't remember exactly what I said to him, but the soldier looked at me dressed in my American uniform, listened, and then got up, swearing, and went to sit down on the verge of the road. After that we were able to continue our way. I was happy and proud to have been of help. I had finally been able to give something back, and it felt as good then as it does today.

Gino felt extremely proud of having been able to do something to help Antonio. Usually, it was the grown-ups who were always helping him, but not that time.

For Gino, family life was very different from a cherished soldiers' mascot. It meant respecting rules and living within limits which he could not have, or at least should not have, gone beyond. Gino remembers a prank which he played when he was still at Coccolia with the Zaccaria family, who were not rich, in fact they had to count every cent.

> *I remember that one day my mummy sent me to buy some things at the grocery store. When I got inside, I saw some licorice candies which I really fancied, so I asked the shopkeeper to give me my change in candy rather than money. She did as I requested and passed over a truly enormous parcel. I realized that I'd really done it this time, but I really wanted those goodies. I just loved the crunch of them between my teeth. I thought it might be better to hide them, so I put them in my grandmother's shed. I don't remember what excuse I made for the missing change, but mom soon discovered the truth. She ordered me to show her where I had hidden the parcel, and then took it back to the shop and demanded her money back. And that certainly wasn't the only prank which I got up to!*

Gino's maternal grandparents were not shy with punishments whenever they felt they were needed. Despite this, Gino was very fond of both Grandpa Pippo and Grandma Maria, even if it was Maria who taught him his first hard lesson. This happened on the very morning that the Americans left Durazzanino, and Gino decided to act up:

> *Grandma Maria spanked me over and over again. She hit me so hard that I almost fell over, then she left me to cry and eventually to fall asleep exhausted on her bed. She felt so guilty that she promised never to hit me again, and I can confirm that she kept her promise.*

Whenever Gino did something that he should not have done, grandpa Pippo ran after him with his belt in his hand, swearing and sometimes taking the Lord's name in vain. Gino was, however, very fond of his grandfather:

He always loved me so much that I would be happy to receive his punishments even now.

When the family moved to Ravenna, Gino caught the bus every Saturday to go to his grandparents' house and spent the weekend with them.

Gino grew healthy and strong with his family, but in the eyes of the law he still did not exist. Fortunately, his complicated circumstances and the concerns of the Farneti family were taken to heart by the Attorney General of Ravenna. The judge searched for a precedent, a previous case like Gino's, which would help them get out of this stalemate. At last, he found one. Rina Farneti recalled:

> *He was very supportive, and he managed to find a similar case: a soldier who during the First World War had managed to adopt a lost child. Despite this precedent, we still could not adopt Gino because we were too young, however we were allowed to become his guardians. The Attorney General conducted a final search for relatives of Gino's in the province of Frosinone, but to no avail. So, he then suggested a compromise solution. Gino was not allowed to take the surname Farneti, but he could be called Farnetti, with an extra T.*

Antonio and Rina decided that Gino's birthday from now on would be on May 10, the day on which the Americans left him at Coccolia before they returned to the United States.

It was not until 1954, ten years after being rescued by the Canadians, that Gino was finally recognized by the authorities. He was no longer invisible and had the right to hold documents. These documents, however, contained uncertain data: date of birth: 1939 (presumed), place of birth: unknown.

As an adult Gino would often travel abroad for work, and these details on his documents would cause problems every time he crossed a border. For him these would be bitter episodes.

'Chow' Until Next Time

FOR THE CANADIANS, THE WAR DID NOT END when they left Italy. They went to France, Belgium, and then Holland. But the soldiers who had spent so much time with Gino continued to think of him. Doug Walker wrote to Mary on March 6, 1945:

No more Italy... You know by now Gino is no longer with us. If he returns, I will let you know. He would have loved paints and a paint book. Thanks again for getting the snaps of Gino. I almost cry when I see them again. He was so dear to us. His friend Red Oliver was acting Papa and believe you me Gino towed the mark when Red told him anything.

In another letter to Mary dated April 2, 1945 he wrote:

Holland. I have been thinking of Gino. I am sure you would have loved him. Especially that glow in his eyes. At times he was a regular rascal. He seemed to get far ahead of his actual age, in his acts. When we first had him, he liked to show off in front of a group of soldiers; but then it got so he wanted to talk and ask questions like youngsters usually do. He was a grand kid, and we miss him so.

At the end of the Second World War Paul Hagen stayed in Europe for two more years. He had been chosen to serve with a military court martial organization defending Canadian service personnel who had been accused of civil law offences under Dutch, Belgian, or French law.

When Paul went home in 1947, he found that Red had not managed to obtain any information about Gino from their few remaining contacts in Italy. Paul also tried to find news of Gino, but without success.

Many of the Canadians who volunteered for the Second World War made this courageous choice, because they felt that they had a moral debt to their fathers, who'd fought in the First World War. Many of them harboured a highly developed sense of justice and freedom, which made the idea of Old Europe falling victim to totalitarianism intolerable.

But in addition to this deep-rooted sense of duty, financial destitution also influenced some in the decision to embrace arms and fight. The Great Depression had brought many North American families to their knees. Many families were large and having a son in the army meant one less person to feed. It was also a secure source of income in dark times. From the end of 1945 onwards, the returning soldiers had to roll up their sleeves and find another way to earn a living for themselves and their families. Consequently, they did not have time or opportunities to stay in touch with their fellow soldiers, who were scattered all over Canada.

As a result, many of them lost track of each other. This was the case with Lloyd "Red" Oliver. In December 1945 he returned to Canada on board the *Queen Elizabeth*. Tony Monti tried to get in touch with him, but Lloyd was not one for writing letters and did not immediately reply. Much later, when Lloyd did finally write, Tony had moved on.

Although he was the soldier who Gino had spent the least time with, when he got home Tony Monti tried repeatedly to have him brought over to the States. Bureaucracy and international laws, however, would not allow it. For a long time, Tony regularly corresponded in Italian with Antonio and Rina Farneti, who kept him up to date on what Gino was doing and how he was growing:

August 15, 1945 - I've been thinking a lot about my Gino, and I even tried to find out how to get him over here when I was in Washington, but everyone told me that I can't bring him over without documents, which obviously we don't have. I hope that his mother is still alive, and that Nino has managed to find something out (...) Please write to me Rina and give me all the news. I hope that we can carry on being friends for years to come. I'll never forget you.

November 17, 1945 – (...) It was wonderful to receive the photograph of my precious Gino. Thank you for everything that you have done for my son who has had so much bad luck. I think about him all the time. I can see from the photograph that he's doing well (...) I'd love to see that cheeky face that I remember so well (...) I've got so much stuff to send to him, but the post office won't accept it yet (...) The Italian government has written that they can't let this child go abroad when the Italian nation has already lost thousands of its young men (...) I'm now waiting for a reply from the American Consul in Florence, and from the American representative from UNNRRA in Rome. If I don't have a positive answer soon, I'll write to Mr Ferruccio Parri."

It was many decades later when Paul Hagen managed to find Gino. In a fifteen-page typed letter to Gino and his family, Paul reconstructed the time they spent together, allowing Gino to put together a few more pieces of the unfinished puzzle.

Life was very different when we got to Belgium. The people there had not had too bad a time from the Germans. We were living in houses with people who had enough to eat. All the stores were open and there were lots of nice things to buy in them which was just the opposite to Italy where we had seen so much hunger and suffering. I thought of you many times and wished that you could be there to see the bright lights and the well-fed comfortable children. Of course, I knew that you were being well cared for; but Army Camps, American or Canadian are not a good playground (parco di giochi) for young five-year-old boys.

We soon moved on into Holland, where things were very bad again, just as bad as it had been in Italy. Lots of hungry people, especially the children. Soon I was glad that you had not come along. The fighting was nearly over but the country had been occupied so long by the Germans that their entire economy was in ruin. There was nothing in the stores or cafes, many people were homeless with a great deal of fighting amongst themselves between people who had been friendly with the Germans and those who had fought for the underground (resistenza partigiani).

Many of my older Buddies, who had been in the Army for more than five years were being sent home to Canada, even before the war ended. I was still young, so I was kept in Holland and did not get my discharge from the army until February of 1947. By that time most of the boys had left the Army and were scattered all over Canada. You have seen how big Canada is, so you realize that it is very difficult to get together or even maintain contact with one another, especially when we had to work long hours to get our lives going again after being away so long at war. I did not hear from Red or any of the other boys for many years. It was only by reading it in the paper that I found out that you had been located and that you had even been to Canada to see Red a few years ago. I sure felt bad that I had missed you!

(...) Both Dorothy and I feel that we have known you all our lives. All my children and grandchildren have heard the story of my little Italian brother many times since they were young. They have also seen me listening to your tapes and they think it is funny that I can understand what you are saying.

Chow until next time. Paul.

Lloyd also never stopped thinking about Gino. For him he was like a first-born son. But it would be thirty years after his return to Canada until he managed to contact the Farneti family and finally see Gino again at a D-Day Dodgers' Reunion in Canada.

Mary and Doug had married in 1947. Many years later, in November 2006, after they had all found each other again, Mary sent Gino a letter and several pages of extracts from the letters which Doug sent her while he was overseas. Each extract contains references to Gino. Mary writes:

I hope it brings back some happy memories. They meant a lot to Doug. For years after the war, he talked about you a great deal (...) You were a gift to them during a trying time in their lives. (...) I always felt I had watch[ed] you grow. You did the boys proud. (...) I hope it brings back some happy memories. For me it was a pleasure to read Doug's letters again. I have a cardboard blanket box full. Nearly 5 years of writing. Love to you all, Mary Walker.

Many of the Veterans, who knew little Gino in those difficult months, kept a photograph of him in their wallet throughout their life. They told their fiancées, wives, children, and grandchildren all about him. Merton Massey never did see Gino again but his daughter, Maureen, sums up how everyone felt:

> *That little boy remained forever in my father's heart and mind. From when I was a little girl, he told me stories about him hundreds of times. Gino was his first-born, and my big brother.*

WITH THE HELP OF A BOOK

THE PAGES OF THE BOOK RAPIDLY TURN until the eyes see what they are looking for. The fingers stop on a photograph with the caption "The Lamone River". Below that, there is the picture of a boy wearing a uniform and the caption:

> *Gino Farnetti, the five-year-old Italian boy who was befriended by truck drivers of the Fifth Canadian Armoured Division. Although the drivers failed in their bid to take Gino with them when they were transferred to northwestern Europe in early 1945, they were able to track him down long after the war and bring him to Canada for reunions in 1980 and again in 1990 (Vic Worley).*

The *Wartime Friends* research group, which was established in 2003 under the umbrella of the University for Adults of Lugo di Romagna, Italy, carries out research into the less well-known aspects of the Second World War. The group is particularly interested in the interaction of soldiers with the local population when allied troops were present along and around the Senio River. They collect testimonies and documents and carry out their investigations with passion and historical rigour. In the course of their work the members of the group have had the chance to meet veterans and their families from all over the world. One of the missions of the group is to accompany these guests on visits to the places where they have fought and to the cemeteries where their loved ones, fellow soldiers and fellow countrymen have been laid to rest. The researchers do this because they recognize the contribution made by people from distant lands for the liberation of Italy, and because they are interested in making a detailed historical reconstruction of what happened in that period.

The group carries out its research tirelessly sieving through documents, books, newspapers, publications, videos, testimonies, and websites. Therefore, when, at the beginning of winter 2009, the book entitled *The D-Day Dodgers: the Canadians in Italy 1943-1945* by Daniel D. Dancocks came into their possession, they immediately started leafing through it. They started at the end and worked back until they found a reference to the Gothic Line, the line of defence erected by the Germans and which passed through the area which they were investigating. It is through this book that the group of researchers met Gino for the first time. Their curiosity aroused, they went through the text looking for further information.

On page 419, a passage told of an attempt by a group of drivers from the Fifth Division to take Gino away with them. *"The orphan had been found at the end of the Liri Valley Campaign by Lloyd Oliver, a Canadian farmer from western Manitoba."* The story continued that the boy was left in the care of a family from Ravenna.

"Ravenna? We'll track him down then!" is what the researchers immediately thought.

They went to the Ravenna town hall, and the register office, but the research which they carried out did not yield results. They could find no trace of Gino Farnetti. Their optimism was dented, but they would not give up at the first obstacle. There was another source which they could turn their attention to: Lloyd "Red" Oliver, the soldier who the book cites as having found little Gino.

The researchers made their first of many intercontinental telephone calls. They got in touch with an existing contact, Jerry Scislowski, the son of Stan, a veteran from the Perth Regiment and author of the book *Not All of Us Were Brave*. They asked Jerry, who lived in Canada, to try and trace Lloyd. He accepted, but was not optimistic: *"Canada is a vast country, and so many years have gone by..."*

In fact, considering all the difficulties involved, the likelihood of success was minimal. Jerry intended to call every Oliver in the phone book in the hope that he would find the needle in the haystack. He dialed the first number on the list and explained to the person who answered that he was looking for a veteran of the Italian Campaign who looked after an Italian orphan during the war.

"That's me!"

Both men were surprised and emotional. Lloyd told Jerry about many of the episodes which he still clearly remembered. Lloyd subsequently sent the research group a written version of the memories which he had put together several years earlier. It included a description of the night in 1944 when Gino, that little orphan who was wandering around all alone in the hills south of Frosinone, crossed the Canadian soldiers' path.

"*It feels like the stars have all lined up to help us on our way in this adventure,*" wrote Jerry in a message dated April 29 of that same year.

Lloyd told the researchers that Gino was now living in a town in the south of Italy, in the province of Foggia. When they heard this the group felt a little discouraged.

> *It was difficult conducting a search in Ravenna, it would be even more difficult looking for him in a place so far away, where we had no contacts. However, we were talking about it during one of our meetings around the kitchen table, when a family member who also happened to be there casually chipped in: 'One of my work colleagues comes from that town.'*

They had already found the needle in the Canadian haystack when Jerry Scislowski traced Lloyd Oliver. No one in the group could imagine being so lucky again. And yet after a couple of weeks, some more research and many phone calls, the person who answered the phone was Gino.

> *The first phone call was deeply moving. Up until then we thought that we would be able to put together the story, but never in our wildest dreams did we expect to meet the main character. It was so exciting and moving to suddenly hear his voice like that.*

It was not long after this first exchange on the telephone that the group got to meet him in person. Gino shared many letters, memories, and photographs that he had carefully kept for decades. The *little soldier boy*, now a grown man, had forgotten most of the English which he spoke so well when he was small. Consequently he did not thoroughly understand the contents of all the materials. The group, therefore, began to patiently transcribe and translate everything that they have been given.

> *It seemed extraordinary to us that we should suddenly have so much material to work on. It documented a fascinating story, which was maybe similar to other wartime stories, but was also unique in that*

there were so many testimonies and illustrated materials. We felt that we had to tell the story and remember the soldiers who took care of Gino. They had demonstrated great humanity, despite strict military rules forbidding them to take such action. We also wanted to remember every person who had been involved in similar episodes and had probably been forgotten.

With the translation of each text, long and deeply buried memories started to come back to Gino. He gradually put together the pieces of the very intricate puzzle that was his life during the war.

There was a steady flow of emails and telephone calls between Gino and the group, and new elements constantly came to light. Details which he remembered, but which he could not fully understand, finally became clear. As the memories came back he recounted them to the group, who then checked them. The researchers found that they did indeed fit in with what they already knew.

Soon it was clear to everyone which pieces of the puzzle were still missing. *"What are Gino's roots? Who were his real parents?"*

This was a painful subject for Gino. It was a wound that had never healed. As an adult, he had never looked into it. He had been put off by circumstance, by his many fears and by all the failed attempts of the early years.

The research group decided to take on the challenge.

THE CIRCLE IS CLOSED

THE FIRST STAGE IN THE SEARCH for Gino's identity was to determine a possible two-year period in which he could have been born. Remembering what Gino said when he was found, the group decided that the period was most likely between June 1938 to June 1940. They researched possible various ways of spelling his surname, including Bragalia, Brogalia, Brigalia, Brighegli, and possible first names, including Gino, Eugenio, Luigi.

They contacted town halls, libraries, dioceses, and the record offices of many towns in the province of Frosinone, but without success. Only from the town of Ceprano did they receive any help. However, this did not produce any results. One of the problems was that it was not clear exactly where Gino was found. Paul Hagen said that it was just south of Frosinone, whilst other sources say it was the area north of Cassino.

Despite the frustrations, another piece of interesting information came to light. During a pleasant conversation at the side of a swimming pool with a couple who lived near Cassino, the researchers asked where the Canadians could have been in late spring 1944, and which towns and villages they might have crossed. Nothing new emerged from this exchange. However, it made them think, and they realized that they had not yet contacted the library in Frosinone: *"Let's call them and see what happens!"*

The group expected nothing useful to come out of this, but were pleasantly surprised. Although it was summertime, the library was open and the staff were happy to help with the research. The library manager put them in touch with an enthusiastic local history research group in Frosinone.

The Wartime Friends group sent these local researchers precise information and excerpts from the veterans' memoirs, which contained clues as to where the events might have taken place. The Frosinone group got down to work.

Gino and a member of the *Wartime Friends* group decided to go to Frosinone in the middle of October. Their intention was to visit some of the record offices and to give Gino the chance to look around and see if anything seemed familiar to him. He had been away for seventy years, but something might strike a chord.

Then came the final unexpected development. Just a few days before the visit to Frosinone, two of the Frosinone researchers received permission to consult the diocese baptism registers. In the large 1938 register, under the letter B, they quickly spotted in Latin: *Ginus ex Bragaglia Giuseppe atque ex Philumena Fiacco*, April 26 at one o'clock in the afternoon. The baby received the sacrament of baptism a week later on May 1, at Torrice in the parish church of San Pietro.

It was him! There was the surname Bragaglia, spelt slightly differently from how it was spelt by Lloyd Oliver and Paul Hagen, but it was him.

At last, the researchers had come into possession of a document which was essential to their reconstruction of Gino's past.

This development was decisive. They immediately went to Torrice and explained what they needed to the leader of the town hall. The staff in the registrar office did not only provide all the help requested, but also had further information which was almost unbelievable. They told the researchers that the grandmother of the register office manager was Gino's family's next-door neighbour. And the old woman was still alive. During those terrible months of 1944 the little boy would often go to her house looking for something to eat. The old lady still remembered Gino, and provided more details about his life before he was abandoned.

All the other information came from other register office documentation about the Bragaglia family. It included new previously unknown details. Gino discovered that he had two older brothers.

The first was Sebastiano, born in 1919, who died in the war on January 3, 1941 in the battle of Bardìa in North Africa.

With his wife, Concetta, Sebastiano had a son who he had never met. He was called Vincenzo and was born in 1941. Concetta and baby Vincenzo lived with Filomena and Gino. This detail helped Gino to understand a memory which up until now he had never been able to explain. *"I remember a cradle at home and pushing it and making it rock back and forth."* Baby Vincenzo died when he was just a few months old, and Gino was three.

Gino was too young to understand what had happened, but his mother was profoundly affected by it. In a period of just two years, Filomena lost a son, a grandson, and also her husband, who was found dead in January 1943. It is very likely that the rapid succession of deaths, the war, and poverty caused Filomena to have a mental breakdown. This was the madness which Gino mentioned to the soldiers when they picked him up.

The other brother, Domenico, was born in 1922. At the beginning of the 1940s, Domenico was perhaps a soldier or had perhaps gone into hiding to avoid having to go to war. For sure, Gino had no memory of him either.

Domenico, who passed away in 1999, had six children, Gino's nieces and nephews. The discovery that three of them had gone to live in Canada was yet another coincidence.

One of the remaining three nephews who had stayed in Italy still lived in Torrice. He lived along the Cervona road in a house built on the very spot where Gino lived as a child. The members of the Frosinone research group organized a visit to the place where Gino's house was. His relatives had gathered there and were looking forward to seeing him. When the car turned into the little road which led to the house, Gino had a sudden flashback, and recognized his surroundings. He was overcome with emotion:

I can see it... I can see the front door, and I push it open... The slope which leads to the field where the broad beans grow... I climb the slope, go down on all fours and crawl into the field to 'steal' some beans so that I can eat something. Mom's there standing in the sun. She's leaning against the wall at the front of the house and she's watching me. I can see her, but I can't make out her face...

Gino sat in the car for a while and tried to compose himself, but when he got out and went to meet his family he was overwhelmed by emotion once again. His mind was now in total confusion. The flashbacks were coming thick and fast. He was dazed and needed to sit down and drink a glass of water. He would need several weeks to come to terms with what had happened. In the meantime he had a growing need to show his gratitude to the men who looked after him during those terrible months which led to the end of the war in Italy. The visit proceeded, and the last pieces of the jigsaw fell into place. He saw the church where he was baptized, and the grave of his parents Giuseppe and Filomena.

In the following weeks the Frosinone research group and the town hall of Torrice organized, for December 16, 2012, an official meeting between Gino and the community of his birth. Representing Canada was Col Tony Battista, Canadian Defence Attaché to Italy. During the extremely touching ceremony Gino was bestowed honorary citizenship of Torrice.

Gino honoured those who saved him all those years ago by planting a maple tree, the maple leaf being a symbol of Canada. It was placed at the junction of what, almost seventy years earlier, the allied military maps designated *Torrice Crossroads*. On May 30, 1944 at this ordinary intersection on the Casilina road, hard-fought and bloody fighting took place between armoured vehicles.

At the foot of the tree a plaque remembers those gallant men:

ON THIS SITE
WHICH OVERLOOKS MY HOME AND THE AREA IN WHICH I WAS
FOUND,
IN THIS SOIL
WHICH RECEIVED THE REMAINS OF NINE CANADIAN SOLDIERS,
THIS MAPLE LEAF,
THE SYMBOL OF CANADA, IS LAID IN MEMORY OF
PAUL HAGEN, LLOYD "RED" OLIVER, AND MERT MASSEY
(Royal Canadian Army Service Corps)
WHO RESCUED AND TOOK CARE OF ME IN JUNE 1944.
MY GRATITUDE GOES TO THEM AND TO ALL THE CANADIANS
WHO
CONTRIBUTED TO RESTORING OUR FREEDOM.

TORRICE, DECEMBER 16, 2012   *GINO BRAGAGLIA*

OPPOSITE: Plaque and Maple Tree at Torrice Crossroads.

Antonio Farneti

Antonio Farneti, capo team della missione "Zella".

Born at Coccolia (RA), Italy on January 7, 1919, he was the third child of a strongly republican family. His mother, Nina, was a farm labourer, and his father, Ottorino, was an accountant at the Coccolia labour cooperative. After primary school Antonio started working in local engineering companies and then joined the aeronautical company Caproni in Forlì as a mechanic.

Since boyhood he believed in republican and anti-fascist ideals. When war broke out he began his clandestine activities by leafleting at the company and setting up a workers' anti-fascist group. He was soon brought to the attention of the fascist militia, was arrested on February 2, 1942 and sent to jail first in Ravenna then in Forlì. After a month he was released and on August 10, 1942 was called up and sent to the Arsenal in Venice. When Mussolini fell on July 25, 1943, Antonio fled from Venice and hid at his sister Rosina's house at Porto Corsini, which was on the coast between Venice and Ravenna. He aimed to immediately start setting up some anti-fascist groups. On August 3 he was declared a deserter. Family and friends persuaded him to return to his unit in Venice, and Antonio did this on August 7. Now back in prison, he was sent to Trieste to be tried by the military court on August 28. Unexpectedly, after a brief interrogation, the trial was adjourned until the end of September and Antonio was sent back to Venice. After September 8 he escaped from Venice and two days later was in Ravenna.

The situation for anti-fascists in non-communist areas was precarious and very disorganized. Antonio took part in some improvised guerrilla activities including attacks on the Garibaldi barracks and on the gunpowder store at Classe. As a result, his group had put together a good stash of weapons and ammunition which were later requisitioned by the communist anti-fascist groups, which were better organized and more disciplined.

Antonio and his six republican friends decided to leave Ravenna and go south with the idea of joining the Allies in the war against the Nazis and Fascists. After many adventures along the way, they arrived in Naples and met Raimondo Craveri, the son-in-law of Benedetto Croce. With his help, they made contact with other anti-fascists and created the Italian Resistance Organization (ORI), which the Americans agreed to absorb into their own military secret service (OSS). The objective was to form small teams and send them into occupied areas of Italy to carry out spying, make contact with local partisan groups, and supply them with arms and other materials. On February 16, 1944 the first team to go out, on an Italian submarine, was the one commanded by Antonio (nom de guerre Roberti). The name of the team was "Zella" and consisted of his friend from Ravenna, Celso Minardi (Benazzi), and his radio operator Andrea Grimaldi (Zanco). Radio Zella would become the first partisan radio to send the Allies more than a hundred messages which, among other things, would allow them to organize numerous air drops of weapons to arm all the partisan brigades.

On July 10, during a round-up in the town of Brisighella, Antonio was arrested, but fortunately not identified as a partisan. He was put in prison in Forlì, but that night he managed to escape and immediately resumed his clandestine activities. Unfortunately, on July 28, 1944 Zanco and the radio were captured by the Germans. As a result, in the following weeks many partisans connected with radio Zella would lose their lives. Zanco would be shot on August 22 in Bologna. Antonio, having left Zanco at Pieve Cesato early in the morning of July 28 to attend a meeting in Lugo, was saved by his fiancée Rina Zaccaria, a partisan runner. Rina had spotted Zanco flanked by two Nazi soldiers in the back of a Jeep near Pieve Cesato. She hurried off to Lugo on her bicycle and warned Antonio, who knew nothing and was on his way back to base.

Despite many attempts by the OSS in the south of Italy to replace the radio set and operator this was not possible. This was why, in October, Antonio decided to cross the front line, which now passed along the ridges of the Apennine mountains, and join the ORI headquarters. Thanks to the help of numerous patriots, Antonio succeeded in his undertaking and on October 28 reached Rome. The Zella mission was officially concluded.

Antonio was attached to the Anglo-American troops and, at the end of November went back to Coccolia where he made contact with some American soldiers from the OSS who were based in a villa near the village. It was here that he met the Italian boy called Gino who had been picked up in the south by Canadian soldiers and then left in the care of American soldiers. The child entered Antonio and Rina's life at the end of the war and would stay with them as their son, even though Italian law would not allow them to officially adopt him.

After the war Antonio and Rina continued to be interested in politics. They sympathized with the communist party, but never actually became members. Soon they married and moved with Gino to Ravenna where Antonio opened a business selling motorbikes and spare parts. This business allowed the family to improve their economic situation. In 1950 the couple had a son, Massimo, who would grow up with Gino and always think of him as his big brother. Gino soon stopped going to school and started working with Antonio, but with his temperament he was better suited to working elsewhere. He went to the ANIC plant, which had recently opened in Ravenna.

In 1960 Antonio and Rina had a daughter, Manuela. By then they were well off, Antonio expanded his business and opened two more stores. Life was good, and busy, and over time he re-established contact with the various American soldiers from the OSS who he knew during the war but had gradually lost touch with. Several times Antonio and Rina flew to the USA to visit their friends, and their friends often came to Italy to stay with them in their home on the outskirts of Ravenna. In 1981 the survivors of the ORI group met up with their old American OSS commanders in Italy. They were received by the Italian president, and presented him with Craveri's book about the ORI group. The years went by and one after another the old friends from the Resistance passed away. In the end, the Farnetis were the only remaining living witnesses of that tragic but stimulating period in the history of Italy and Romagna. On February 22, 2009, at the grand old age of ninety, still very much involved in his spare parts stores, Antonio suddenly died. Exactly sixty-five years earlier, on February 22, 1944, Antonio came ashore from his submarine to make his contribution to the liberation of Italy from nazism-fascism.

PAUL HAGEN

Born to parents Knute and Elnora Hagen on September 5, 1923 in Minot, North Dakota, USA. His father emigrated from Norway and his mother was born in Canada. When Paul was nine months old, his family moved to the province of Saskatchewan in Canada to be closer to his maternal grandparents. Paul was fifth in a family of eleven children. Being one of the older children he learned early how to be a big brother.

Living through the Great Depression was difficult. His family moved back and forth between Saskatchewan and Manitoba with Paul attending school mainly in Winnipeg. He was about fourteen years old when his family moved to northern Manitoba to try their hand at farming.

In 1941, Paul enlisted in the Canadian Army in Regina, Saskatchewan. He was not able to leave for Europe until he was eighteen and a half years old. He was first billeted in Britain, then went by ship to Sicily and the Italian mainland where Paul and Ike Klassen found Gino. They took young Gino back to their camp where many of the soldiers nurtured and cared for him until their next deployment one year later. Paul continued with the Canadian Corps through France, Belgium, Holland, and Germany and returned home in 1947.

After trying his hand at a variety of different jobs, Paul applied for work as an apprentice with Bennett Electric where he became a journeyman electrician. Paul had an insatiable appetite for knowledge and took night classes and correspondence courses where he learned about automatic controls for temperature, pressure, steam, water, and air handling. He eventually became an electrical contractor and worked in the installation and maintenance of commercial gas and oil burners. He had both oil and gas fitters' licenses.

Paul married Dorothy and they had three children: Evelyn, Chris, and Mark, followed by grandchildren and his darling great-granddaughter Olivia, whose name always brought a cheery smile to his face.

Paul became a born-again Christian in 1962 and was very active with his local church. He worked with young boys at a Hunter Safety Club which included Bible study and first-aid. He taught Sunday school to young teenage boys and then involved them in musical activities at his family's home. During the summers Paul worked as a counsellor at Bible Camp.

In 1970, Paul was hired by the Government of Manitoba to work as an electrical inspector. When it was discovered he had training not only in the electrical field but also in heating, Paul took on multiple roles as electrical, gas, and oil inspector which involved traveling extensively to all corners of the province. Eventually, Paul was selected to become the supervisor of inspectors, because of his background with boilers, as well as electrical, gas, and oil. While working for the Department of Labour with the Manitoba government, Paul served on a variety of committees both provincially and federally.

Paul retired from the civil service in January 1989, but remained active in various areas of the industry. He had a well-equipped machine and welding shop on his hobby farm where he built and created a variety of machines.

In his later years, Paul became actively involved in trying to better the plight of seniors. For several years he worked on an advisory committee for the provincial government, worked on a policy committee for a political party, and worked on a weekly radio program which was run by seniors for seniors.

Paul's entire life was devoted to trying to better mankind and to leave this world a safer, kinder, and more equal place for all.

Paul passed away on June 4, 2011.

MERTON MASSEY

Born in Killerney, Manitoba, Canada on July 29, 1916. His father was from Merton, England, went to school at Oxford, then emigrated to Canada where he met and married May Fawler. They lived on a farm and had five children, Mert being the oldest boy.

In 1938 Mert enlisted in the Canadian Army and went overseas. He was in England, Italy, and Holland during the war.

During his time in Italy, Mert wrote many poems. He liked writing and, according to his best friend, Lloyd Oliver, was able to write poems about everything. When Gino was taken in by his unit the *little soldier boy* became the favourite subject of his rhymes.

In England Mert met Elisabeth Brown, and they were married on August 15, 1945, the first day of peace. They were to be married earlier but there was a gale on the English Channel and he was not able to get to England. He went back to Canada and his spouse followed. Mert was a mechanic. He owned his own garage briefly and then worked at a lumber mill as a maintenance foreman until he retired at the age of sixty-five. On December 1, 1953, his daughter Maureen was born. She was the apple of his eye. Later on his days were brightened by the birth of his grandchildren, who he was very fond of. He taught them how to grow vegetables, one of his favourite pastimes. Mert told his daughter about Gino, who always thought of him as her big brother.

Mert died on December 23, 1989, one year after losing his much-loved wife.

TONY MONTI

Born on August 5, 1919 at LaGrange, Illinois, USA, Tony was the son of Italian parents: Giuseppe from Sicily, and Angelina from Calabria. Like many other Italians, his parents had emigrated to the United States in search of a better life. Tony, who had an older brother called Frank, attended school in the US and learned the English language, but at home he continued to speak Italian.

In 1940, he married Lois Stedniz and they settled in New Mexico. When war broke out, he enrolled in the American Army, and as he was a first-generation immigrant who knew the language, culture, and attitudes of his parents' country of origin, he was chosen to join a special organization called the Office of Strategic Services (OSS), formed in 1942. Tony was first sent to Africa and then to Italy. He was a radio operator, his unit working alongside the British 8th Army. It was while he was stationed at the British headquarters in Cattolica that he met Gino, who was camped nearby with his new soldier companions. They met again several months later, and Tony looked after the little boy until he went home at the end of the conflict in 1945. While in Italy, Tony also met Antonio Farneti and Rina. They became firm friends and this continued with correspondence, meetings, and even holidays spent together, for the whole of their lives.

When he returned to civilian life, Tony went to work at General Motors Corporation as a manager in the repairs department, and he stayed there for the rest of his working life.

In his free time he enjoyed acting in theatre, playing sport, and fishing. Most of his time, however, was spent on his Ham Radio which he used to speak to the whole world. It was because of his skill with the radio, as well as his knowledge of two languages, that he had been chosen for the OSS.

Tony and Lois had two children, Michael and Susan, and later on had six grandchildren, and then six great-grandchildren.

Tony died in Albuquerque, New Mexico on February 23, 2006.

LLOYD REGINALD OLIVER

Born on February 25, 1923 in Miniota, Manitoba, Canada. His father, Reginald, ran the town newspaper and his mother, Lillian, kept the

house. He had two sisters, Ruth and Shirley. As a child he went to school in Miniota and then helped his family on the farm.

On July 14, 1939 a call came out for men to join the army and Lloyd decided, along with a few of his friends, to join up. He soon went to Camp Shilo, Manitoba for a month and then was moved to Camp Borden in Ontario. He was there all winter, which he liked, as it was warmer than Shilo. When spring came he was moved to better camp billets and started training in truck driving. Just over a year after this training, he was sent to England. He spent two years there and then went to Italy. From Italy, he traveled to France, Belgium, and then Holland for the Liberation. After that, he was sent to Oldenburg, Germany. After the war ended, he returned to Canada on December 1945 aboard the Queen Elizabeth ship.

He returned to Miniota, bought some land, and started farming. Winters were sometimes slow so he headed for Sault Ste Marie, Ontario to work on the railroad. In 1951, Lloyd married Beth Lorimer, a registered nurse from Pope, Manitoba. They built a house south of Miniota and raised seven children: Dennis, Paul, Brian, Darcy, Ted, Julia, and Betty.

He enjoyed living in Miniota and all the things rural life had to offer. For many years he was known as "Mr. Fix-it," building houses, digging wells, etc. as his off-the-farm job.

In 1978, Lloyd and other veterans took part in a pilgrimage to Italy.

He wanted to try and trace Gino. With the help of many people, he managed to contact the Farneti family in Ravenna, but Gino, now an adult, was abroad for work. Now that he had his address, Lloyd wrote to Gino and Gino wrote back. This is how they met once again after being torn apart so many years before. Gino's old comrades all decided to invite him to Canada, so they could see him again and give him a big hug now that he was a grown man. From that day on, Gino would regularly exchange letters and telephone calls with his soldier friends.

In his late years Lloyd said:

In my 89 years I have seen and experienced many things locally and internationally. If I had any advice to give I would say: 'Always be friendly and willing to work. Be good to your family and friends, the rest will take care of itself.'

Lloyd died on July 6, 2013 and during the eulogy at his funeral, a piece was read out which Gino had sent from Italy.

DOUGLAS STANLEY WALKER

Walker was born in Preston, Ontario, Canada on March 11, 1920. His father, Arnold Spencer, and his mother, Merle Colbeck, met at Batley, Yorkshire, during the First World War. Arnold was a Canadian soldier. At the end of the war, Merle followed him to Canada where they married and settled in Preston.

Doug was very athletic when he attended high school and competed in field events such as high jump and long jump (broad jump). His favourite sport had always been baseball, and it remained his passion until he died. Approximately one year after graduating high school, Doug enlisted as a volunteer in the Army. He went to England first, for basic training. Then he was sent to Italy via ship. On the way, the convoy was in the Mediterranean when it was attacked by U-boats. The hospital ship in front of Doug's ship was torpedoed. Ships were not allowed to travel alone due to the dangers involved. When they stopped to pick up survivors, the rest of the flotilla went ahead without them, so they docked in North Africa, and waited for the next flotilla to arrive. Instead of going to Sicily first, he went directly to mainland Italy. He landed in the south, and from there the troops worked their way to Ortona, then to the Liri Valley and up into the Lombard plain. They fought for about a year and a half. Doug was a proud member of the D-Day Dodgers, a group of Canadian soldiers fighting in Italy who didn't participate in the invasion of France and were apparently much maligned for this by Lady Astor in the British houses of parliament. She described them as the lazy Canadians who were lounging on the Italian beaches drinking wine, while in fact they were involved in some of the toughest fighting of the war, managing to prevent the Nazis from sending larger numbers of troops to the Allied landing in Normandy. There were 25,000 Canadian casualties with 6,000 fatalities.

When victory and peace finally came to Europe, the Canadians had to wait their turn to return home. Doug spent this period going to the University of Ghent in Belgium. He really enjoyed his time there. He finally made it home to Preston in the spring of 1946. He planned on going on to university, but a good friend who had a printing business talked him into coming to work for him, so Doug
would embark on his career as a hot lead typesetter at Progress Printing. He would spend forty years there before he finally set up a business on his own in the mid 1970s. He is proud to say that he was a compositor in the printing industry.

He married Mary on June 4, 1947 and they had four children: Wendy, Douglas, Jeffrey, and Andrew.

In the years following the war, Doug lost touch with many of his fellow soldiers. Later in his life Ernie Kane of Orillia, ON informed him that there was going to be a reunion of the D-Day Dodgers. Doug attended several of these reunions and happily reacquainted himself with many old friends. His biggest pleasure was when Gino attended and they spent some time getting to know each other again after so many years. Doug was so proud of how Gino had succeeded in life after such a tumultuous beginning. Doug and Mary's children and grandchildren all knew about Doug's story in Italy with Gino and took a great interest in him.

Doug passed away on May 27, 1990.

RINA ZACCARIA

Born in Coccolia (Ra), Italy on June 28, 1922. She was the only daughter of Giuseppe, a bricklayer, and Maria Andreini, housewife and community helper. Giuseppe, who was a passionate republican, refused to join the fascist party. Consequently, he could not find work and would be forced to emigrate to Zara on the other side of the Adriatic Sea. When she finished elementary school, Rina had to start work, because her family was struggling to make ends meet. She became a seamstress first in Forlì, and then in Ravenna. She was good at her job and was soon bringing home a wage, which was an important help to the family. At the age of fifteen she fell in love with Antonio Farneti, who was a few years older than her. And it was love which drove her to join the anti-fascist movement. She started out distributing leaflets here and there, and then became increasingly involved. After September 8, 1943, Antonio, who was now her fiancé, left to join the resistance movement in the south. By this time, Rina had become an antifascist activist. Antonio came back to Romagna in February 1944, and under the nom de guerre 'Roberti' was now commander of the Italian Resistance Organization's (ORI) radio mission Zella. Rina became the most reliable and constant link between the ORI and the anti-fascists in Romagna, especially republican anti-fascists. Part of her life was 'regular' and part of it was spent working as a partisan runner. She often slept away from home in various houses which secretly helped partisans in the area around Faenza and was always near her commander Roberti. She told her mother she was staying with friends or distant relatives. Her father, on the other hand, knew what was going on, and helped his daughter in her semi-clandestine life.

On July 10, 1944 the commander of the ORI partisan brigade, Antonio Bellenghi, and his second-in-command, Bruno Neri, were killed in action at Gamogna (Fi). Radio Zella, which was based in the Neri family's villa near Faenza, was no longer safe. Rina took charge of moving the radio, which had been taken apart, placed in some jars, and covered in jam. She set off on her bicycle with two large bags hanging from the handlebar and another across her body. She was escorted from a distance by two partisans. Rina took the radio to a safe place, the farm in Pieve Cesato belonging to the anti-fascist Pietro Fabbri. On the way, she had to cross the Lamone River, but the bridge had collapsed. Two young German soldiers helped her across on a small boat. She was young and good-looking and, for the cause, was willing to accept some heavy flirting.

A few days later, the situation worsened. The Germans captured Zanco, the mission's radio operator. Rina was going from Coccolia to Pieve Cesato to tell Antonio that his father, Ottorino, had been arrested when, by chance, she met the Jeep which was taking Zanco to the German headquarters. She realized what was happening. Thinking that Antonio might also have been arrested, she fainted at the side of the road and was helped by some refugees. As soon as she recovered consciousness, she thought of

"Nonna" Maria and "Nonno" Pippo with Gino.

Antonio, got back on her bicycle, and quickly but warily cycled to Pieve Cesato and the house of a collaborator. From him she learned that Antonio had spent the night at the Fabbri family's farm, and had left early in the morning for an important meeting in Lugo. There were at least two roads which connected Pieve Cesato and Lugo, and luckily Rina chose the same road that Antonio had chosen to return on. She met him, told him to stay away from the Fabbris' house, and so saved his life. The capturing of Zanco and the radio marked the end of the Zella mission and led to the killing of numerous partisans and anti-fascists. One of the killed was Pietro Fabbri who gave himself up in order to save the rest of his family, who would otherwise have been shot as a reprisal. A few weeks later, Antonio joined the Allies, who were slowly moving north. Rina went back to her 'regular' life, but had to wait until November and the liberation of her village to see her Antonio again. One day Antonio brought her a little boy who had been living with the Americans of the OSS, stationed at a villa outside Coccolia. More and more often little Geng spent his days at the Zaccaria family's house with grandpa Pippo and grandma Maria. Gino soon learned Italian and the local dialect. On May 10, the OSS operatives had to return home, and they left Gino in the care of Rina and Antonio, who would bring him up as a son. From that moment on, the lives of Rina, Antonio and Gino were bound together as they became the Farneti family. Rina and Antonio remained united until Sunday, February 22, 2009. On that day, the sixty-fifth anniversary of Radio Zella's landing in the mouth of the Po River, Antonio left his Rina forever, passing away at the age of ninety.

Rina still had the love of her three children, Gino, Massimo, and Manuela, and of her grandchildren, but she had other trials to face, the hardest being illness. This exceptional woman passed away at the age of ninety-one on September 13, 2013. Rina lived through some of the most tragic and intense periods of Italy's recent history. She belonged to that generation who gave the Italian people freedom after the darkness of fascism.

SOURCES

BOOKS

Cederberg, F., *The Long Road Home: The Autobiography of a Canadian Soldier in Italy in World War II*, Toronto 2000.

Clifton, B., *Dear Mom and Pop: The Overseas Letters of Private Penny*, Lethbridge, Alberta 2012.

Dancocks, D.G., *The D-Day Dodgers: the Canadians in Italy 1943-45*, Toronto 1991.

Frost, S.F., *Once a Patricia*, St. Catharines: Vanwell Publishing, 1988.

Guberti P., *I Romagnoli si raccontano-memorie resistenziali*, Ed. Stear, Ravenna, 1985.

Jadecola, C., *I giorni della Hitler. Maggio 1944: quando la Valle del Liri divenne un inferno*, Castrocielo (Fr), 2009.

Johnston, S., *The Fighting Perths*, Ontario, 1964.

Nicholson, G.W.L., *Official History of the Canadian Army in the Second World War, II, The Canadians in Italy, 1943-1945*, Ottawa 1957.

O'Donnell, P., *Operatives, Spies, and Saboteurs: The Unknown Story of the Men and Women of WWII's OSS*, New York: Free Press, 2004.

Scislowski, S., *Not All of Us Were Brave*, Toronto 1997.

Tompkins, P., *L'altra Resistenza, il Saggiatore*, Milan 2005.

Weckstein, L., *200,000 Heroes*, Ashland: Hellgate Press, 2011.

LETTERS AND INTERVIEWS

Bragaglia Gino., private conversation between Mariangela Rondinelli, 2009-2014.

Farneti, Rina., private conversation with Mariangela Rondinelli, 2010.

Hagen, P., private letter to Gino, 23.12.1992.
Hagen, P., private correspondence with Mariangela Rondinelli, 2009-2010.

Marcolla, J., private correspondence with Rina Farneti, 1945-1946.
Monti, T., private correspondence with Rina Farneti, 1945-1946.

Oliver, L., private correspondence with family and Gino, 1944-2011.
Oliver, L., private correspondence with Mariangela Rondinelli, 2009-2011.

Walker, D., extracts from private correspondence with his girlfriend Mary, 1944-1945.

OFFICIAL DOCUMENTS

Baptism certificate of Gino Bragaglia, drawn up by Don Egidio Vincenzi, preserved in the diocese of Frosinone.
Extract from the 9th population census (1951), released by the Municipality of Torrice.
The Irish Regiment of Canada War Diary, January-February 1945.
Summary extract of the birth certificate of Luigi Bragaglia, issued by the Municipality of Torrice.

ARTICLES

"He's Corporal Gino Now," *The Winnipeg Evening Tribune*, Thursday, Feb.8, 1945.
"Canuck Adopts Italian War Orphan," *The Globe and Mail*, 23 May 1945.
"Un bambino biondo con gli occhi neri," *Il Rapido*, Year I, Number 3, 17 December 1945.
"Verso l'identificazione del bambino biondo ospitato a Coccolia?," *Il*

Rapido, Year II, Number 3, 11 February 1946.

"Un bambino ricerca i familiari nel Cassinate," *La Gazzetta Ciociara*, 22 December *1953*.

"Un ragazzo di quattordici anni è nato ufficialmente da due mesi," *Il Carlino Sera*, 8 March 1954.

"La Mascotte dei Canadesi," *Oggi*, 1 April 1954.

Our Special Thanks

WE WISH TO OFFER OUR SPECIAL THANKS to Mr. Gino Farnetti-Bragaglia who kindly made available to us his paper materials, photos, his memories, those of his adoptive mother, the Canadians involved in his affair and who followed, step by step, the reconstruction of the events.

In addition to Gino, and all the people mentioned in the text, we would like to extend our heartfelt thanks to the group of researchers from Frosinone: Gianni Blasi, Maurizio Federico, Costantino Jadecola, Paolo Maria Sbarbada.

We would also like to thank: Anna Bagnaresi, Gordon Bannerman, Angelo D'Agostino, Michele Falcone, Massimo and Manuela Farneti, Deanna Geminiani, Evelyn and Dorothy Hagen, Giuseppe Masetti, Michael Monti, Daniele Morelli, Maureen Mousseau, Brian Oliver, Ernesto Raio, Katia Savo, Jerry Scislowski, Fabio Solaroli, Riccardo Tesse, Antonio Valgimigli, and Jeff and Drew Walker.

Both Karen Storwick and Tony Battista have been instrumental in presenting this story to Canadian audiences, both through film and this book. They have our deepest thanks.

And finally, our very special thanks to Prof. Francesco Dalla Valle, honorary president of Lugo (Ra) University for Adults, for his continuous encouragement.

Photo Gallery

ON AUGUST 10, 1944, while away from her husband who was engaged on the Italian front, Mary Walker noted in her diary, "Doug sent me Gino's negatives. I made 100 prints of each. There are at least 300, everyone wanted them. He had collected the money, then went to Rome and spent it all." Years later, Mary, who had financed the prints, still remembers that episode, "We were married for 42 years and I often teased him about that money he owed me from his time in Italy."

There are many photographs taken of Gino during that period. This is unusual, considering the years and circumstances. Three in particular use the camera to capture their mascot's smiles-Paul Hagan, Doug Walker and, later, Tony Monti.

An entire year, from June 1944 to June of the following year, in which Gino becomes the protagonist of every image.

The photo gallery in this book offers some of those shots, recovered thanks to the collaboration of all those who participated directly and indirectly in the collection of materials.

Doug Walker with Gino, Ravenna, 1945.

ABOVE: Gino on a destroyed German "Tiger" Tank with Lorin Kenny.
BELOW": Gino with Lorin Kenny.

Gino with Peter Skyrzyk.

Gino on the running board of Tony Monti's truck.

Gino with Paul Hagen.

From left to right, Red Oliver, Gino, and Peter Skyrzyic. (front and back of photo)

SEPT. 1944

The little chevron on the right sleeve means he's going on his 5th year overseas. I don't want them thanks.

H

RED
LLOYD OLIVER
FARNETTI.
JINO BRAGALIA

PETER SKgRZyIC

THE TRUCK WAS

TONy MONTIS
PICTURE TAKEN WHEN
TONy VISITED US

'WARTIME FRIENDS' Research Group
BAGNACAVALLO (RA)
www.wartimefriends.org

Wartime Friends is a research group founded in 2003, on the personal and spontaneous initiative of several enthusiasts, as part of the Lugo (Ra) Adult University. The group's headquarters is in Bagnacavallo (Ra), a small town in Romagna near the Senio River front, liberated on Dec. 21, 1944, by Canadian troops.

The research group studies minor aspects related to the presence of Allied troops, on the Senio front and adjacent areas, during the Second World War. Particular attention is given to the relationships and interaction of the military with the local population. All activities of the Wartime Friends are carried out during free time, in a completely voluntary manner, in an atmosphere of friendship and cooperation, with the only gain being personal satisfaction and commitment to a worthy cause: the desire to preserve and enhance the memory and testimonies relating to a period, as tragic as it was intense and, at the same time, the deep feeling of gratitude towards the contribution made by the Allies to liberation.

Over the years, the Wartime Friends have met with numerous Veterans and their families, sharing information, accompanying them on visits to battle sites and to military cemeteries where their loved ones, fellow soldiers or compatriots rest. Particularly dear to the group is the Canadian cemetery in Villanova di Bagnacavallo: the Wartime Friends collaborate in official ceremonies on liberation anniversaries.

The group maintains intense relations with other 'Wartime Friends' from abroad, particularly from Canada and the United Kingdom, and welcomes exchange and collaboration with other enthusiasts from Italy and all over the world.

The project the research group is currently working on is the collection of biographical data and photographs of the 212 fallen soldiers buried at the Canadian cemetery in Villanova di Bagnacavallo.

The Wartime Friends have over the years produced multimedia works on DVD related to aspects of the war in the Bagnacavallo area: Wartime Friends (2004, a tribute to John Thurlby and Alan Woods, materials and testimonies on Bagnacavallo in 1944/45); Riding on Memories: from the Lamone to the Senio (2005, on the footsteps of the Canadian Perth Regiment in the Bagnacavallo area); Riding on Stan's Memories (2006, a tribute to Stan Scislowsky's account). In 2006 they produced the exhibition "In Sunny Italy". Wartime Vignettes, the result of the collection and study of humorous cartoons drawn by W.J.P. Jones and W. Coughlin for the British and Canadian military. The exhibition was inaugurated in December 2006 in Bagnacavallo and successfully repeated several times as part of various cultural and commemorative initiatives: in Lugo di Romagna (spring 2007), Villanova di Bagnacavallo (2007), Stone and Stafford in the United Kingdom (November 2007), Cervia (2009), and Traversara di Bagnacavallo (2014). A bilingual printed catalog (2009) and DVD (2006) "In Sunny Italy" was published with the exhibition.

DOUBLE‡DAGGER
— www.doubledagger.ca —

Double Dagger Books is Canada's only military-focused publisher. Conflict and warfare have shaped human history since before we began to record it. The earliest stories that we know of, passed on as oral tradition, speak of war, and more importantly, the essential elements of the human condition that are revealed under its pressure.

We are dedicated to publishing material that, while rooted in conflict, transcend the idea of "war" as merely a genre. Fiction, non-fiction, and stuff that defies categorization, we want to read it all.

Because if you want peace, study war.